World Heritage Site Top 38

By Nina Wegner

Level 5

IBC パブリッシング

はじめに

　ラダーシリーズは、「はしご（ladder）」を使って一歩一歩上を目指すように、学習者の実力に合わせ、無理なくステップアップできるよう開発された英文リーダーのシリーズです。

　リーディング力をつけるためには、繰り返したくさん読むこと、いわゆる「多読」がもっとも効果的な学習法であると言われています。多読では、「1. 速く 2. 訳さず英語のまま 3. なるべく辞書を使わず」に読むことが大切です。スピードを計るなど、速く読むよう心がけましょう（たとえば TOEIC® テストの音声スピードはおよそ1分間に150語です）。そして1語ずつ訳すのではなく、英語を英語のまま理解するくせをつけるようにします。こうして読み続けるうちに語感がついてきて、だんだんと英語が理解できるようになるのです。まずは、ラダーシリーズの中からあなたのレベルに合った本を選び、少しずつ英文に慣れ親しんでください。たくさんの本を手にとるうちに、英文書がすらすら読めるようになってくるはずです。

《本シリーズの特徴》

- 中学校レベルから中級者レベルまで5段階に分かれています。自分に合ったレベルからスタートしてください。
- クラシックから現代文学、ノンフィクション、ビジネスと幅広いジャンルを扱っています。あなたの興味に合わせてタイトルを選べます。
- 巻末のワードリストで、いつでもどこでも単語の意味を確認できます。レベル1、2では、文中の全ての単語が、レベル3以上は中学校レベル外の単語が掲載されています。
- カバーにヘッドホーンマークのついているタイトルは、オーディオ・サポートがあります。ウェブから購入／ダウンロードし、リスニング教材としても併用できます。

《使用語彙について》

レベル1：中学校で学習する単語約1000語

レベル2：レベル1の単語＋使用頻度の高い単語約300語

レベル3：レベル1の単語＋使用頻度の高い単語約600語

レベル4：レベル1の単語＋使用頻度の高い単語約1000語

レベル5：語彙制限なし

INTRODUCTION

Our world is full of treasures. Whether it is a unique landscape, a natural environment, or a historical building, every country in the world has some rare traits to share. These sites teach people everywhere to appreciate the interesting places and incredible variety of nature, culture, and history that exists on our planet.

World Heritage Committee, which recognizes World Heritage Sites, is a branch of the United Nations Educational, Scientific, and Cultural Organization (UNESCO). Since 1972, when the World Heritage Committee was created, it has recognized World Heritage Sites in 160 countries throughout the world. These sites are recognized as either a cultural site or a natural site, but sometimes a site will be considered to hold mixed value.

A site becomes officially recognized after a very specific process. First, a country must study its unique properties and make a list of possible World Heritage Sites. Next, the country can select a site or property from the list to nominate as a World Heritage Site. This site is reviewed by two organizations, the International Council on Monuments and Sites and the World

Conservation Union. These two organizations make a recommendation to the World Heritage Committee. Then, the World Heritage Committee meets once a year to make a decision on whether the selected sites should be officially recognized as World Heritage Sites.

There are ten criteria that are used to select a World Heritage Site. A site must meet at least one of them to become officially recognized. Once a place becomes a World Heritage Site, the home country is responsible for protecting and preserving the site as best as it can, so that it can be appreciated by the whole world for years to come. However, some World Heritage Sites are considered to be in danger due to wars and conflicts in the home country, environmental threats, development, or other reasons.

The names given for the places in this book are the official UNESCO names for each site. The country that houses the site is given after the name. You'll find that some of these places are combinations of several monuments and historical sites, and some are shared between countries across borders. Some are sites of mixed value, with both cultural and natural lessons to teach the world. All of these sites show unique value and are appreciated by millions from many nations.

Contents

INTRODUCTION 1

AFRICA — 7

Kunta Kinteh Island and Related Sites, Gambia 8
Memphis and Its Necropolis—the Pyramid Fields
    from Giza to Dahshur, Egypt 10
Mosi-oa-Tunya/Victoria Falls National Park,
    Zambia and Zimbabwe 12
Serengeti National Park, Tanzania 13
Timbuktu, Mali 15

ASIA — 17

Ancient City of Damascus, Syrian Arab Republic 18
Angkor, Cambodia 19
Buddhist Monuments in the Horyu-ji Area, Japan 21
Fuji-san, Sacred Place and Source of Artistic Inspiration, Japan 22
The Great Wall, China 24
Lumbini, Birthplace of the Lord Buddha, Nepal 26
Mausoleum of the First Qin Emperor, China 27
Old City of Jerusalem and Its Walls, Jerusalem District 29
Old City of Sana'a, Yemen 31
Petra, Jordan 33
Taj Mahal, India 35

AUSTRALIA & OCEANIA — 37

Great Barrier Reef, Australia 38
Kakadu National Park, Australia 39

Phoenix Islands Protected Area, Kiribati..41
Tongariro National Park, New Zealand...42

EUROPE 45

Acropolis, Athens, Greece..46
Auschwitz Birkenau German Nazi Concentration
  and Extermination Camp (1940-1945), Poland.................................47
Hierapolis-Pamukkale, Turkey...49
Historic Center of the City of Salzburg, Austria......................................50
Historic Fortified City of Carcassonne, France..52
Mont Saint-Michel and its Bay, France..53
Stonehenge, Avebury and Associated Sites, United Kingdom............55
Venice and Its Lagoon, Italy...57

NORTH & CENTRAL AMERICA 59

Canadian Rocky Mountain Parks, Canada..60
Grand Canyon National Park, USA..61
Maya Site of Copán, Honduras..63
Old Havana and Its Fortifications, Cuba..65

SOUTH AMERICA 67

Galápagos Islands, Ecuador...68
Historic Sanctuary of Machu Picchu, Peru..70
Iguazu National Park, Argentina and Brazil..72
Los Glaciares National Park, Argentina...74
Port, Fortresses, and Group of Monuments, Cartagena, Colombia....76
Rapa Nui National Park, Chile..78

Word List..80

読みはじめる前に

本書で使われている用語です。わからない語は巻末のワードリストで確認しましょう。

- □ ancient
- □ archaeologist
- □ architecture
- □ cliff
- □ ecosystem
- □ empire
- □ fort
- □ heritage
- □ mosque
- □ prehistoric
- □ represent
- □ ruin
- □ slave
- □ statue
- □ tomb
- □ waterfall

地域別登録数とその特徴

【アフリカの世界遺産】

アフリカ大陸では134件の世界遺産が登録されており、そのうち、17件が危機遺産に指定されています。アフリカは人類発祥の地とも言われます。サハラ砂漠より北は、エジプト、リビアを中心に中東の一部と定義されることもあり、多くの人がイスラム教を信仰しています。ローマ帝国の支配も受けたため、ローマの遺跡なども数多く残っています。

【アジアの世界遺産】

アジアでは243件の世界遺産が登録されており、15件が危機遺産です。最も深刻なのは、シリアで、登録している世界遺産6件、すべてが危機遺産になっています。これは、2011年より続いている反政府運動と政府軍の武力衝突（シリア騒乱）が原因です。

【ヨーロッパの世界遺産】

ヨーロッパ諸国の世界遺産は448件です。イタリア（49件）とスペイン（44件）だけで、100件近くの遺産を保有していま

す。長い歴史と伝統の中で生み出された遺産は他を圧倒する数と質を誇っています。

【オセアニアの世界遺産】

オセアニア地域では29件の世界遺産があります。ソロモン諸島のレンネル島の一部、東レンネルは、世界で最も大きな珊瑚島ですが、森林伐採が進み、現在は危機にさらされている世界遺産とされています。

【北米・中米の世界遺産】

北米から中米にかけ102件の世界遺産があります。メソアメリカ地域では紀元前1500年前後には文明が誕生し、メキシコにはマヤ文明の遺跡なども多くの文化遺産が残っています。

【南米の世界遺産】

南米には67件の世界遺産が登録されています。南米の多くの国が南半球に位置しています。なかでもアマゾン川流域に拡がるアマゾン盆地は広大で、熱帯雨林が密集し、周辺には「中央アマゾン保全地域群」や「パンタナル保全地域」などがあります。

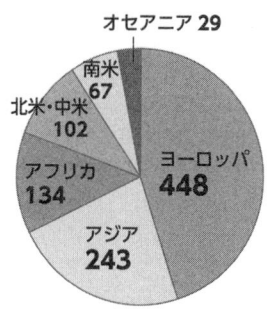

(2013年6月現在)
出典：UNESCO World Heritage Centre

AFRICA

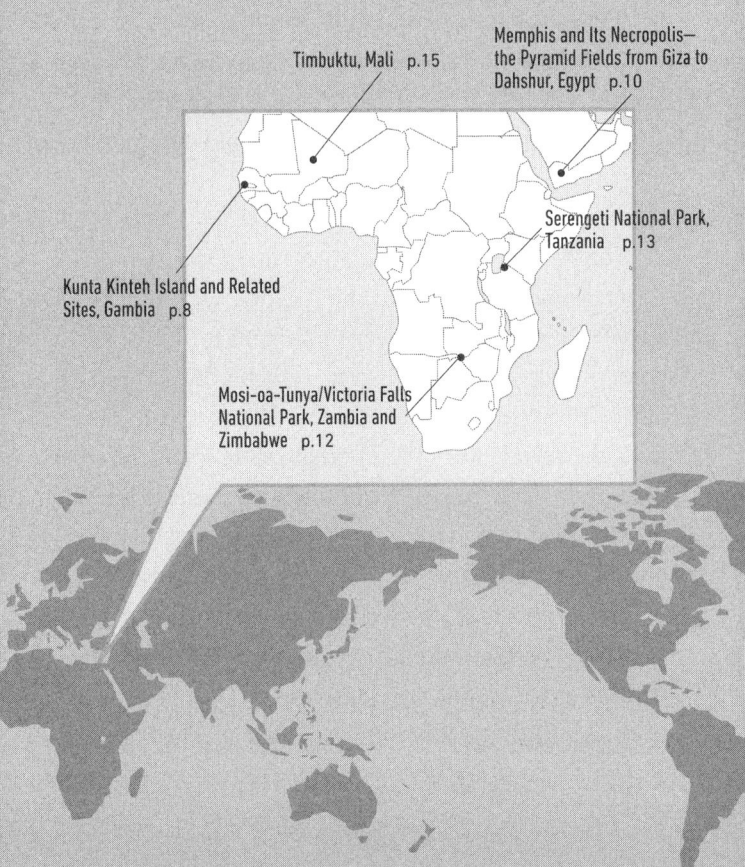

Timbuktu, Mali p.15

Memphis and Its Necropolis—
the Pyramid Fields from Giza to
Dahshur, Egypt p.10

Serengeti National Park,
Tanzania p.13

Kunta Kinteh Island and Related
Sites, Gambia p.8

Mosi-oa-Tunya/Victoria Falls
National Park, Zambia and
Zimbabwe p.12

Kunta Kinteh Island and Related Sites, Gambia
Cultural World Heritage Site since 2003

Many World Heritage Sites have deep historical and cultural importance, but sometimes the memories they bring up are painful ones. Kunta Kinteh Island and Related Sites in Gambia is an example of just such a painful site—the island holds deep historical value, but the stories it tells are about some of the most terrible deeds in history. They are stories of the African slave trade.

Kunta Kinteh Island is located on the Gambia River, which runs toward the Atlantic Ocean. It is a small island, but it was very important for European traders because of its position, which allowed quick access to African goods. The first Europeans to take over the island were the Portuguese in 1456. However, the island passed from one European country to another over the next two centuries, finally ending up under British rule in the mid-1600s.

The island and its river helped form one of the first trade routes through Africa. At first, European traders moved ivory and gold on the Gambia River to the ships that waited in the Atlantic. These ships

would then take the goods back to Europe. Then, from roughly the 17th century, the goods that were carried down the river changed. The traders using the river and the island began to deal in humans—in African slaves.

This World Heritage Site consists of seven different sites. These are Kunta Kinteh Island, the ruins of a Portuguese church, an old warehouse, the Maurel Frères Building, the ruins of a small Portuguese trading village, Fort Bullen, and the Six-Gun Battery. These sites are located in various spots along the river within 30 kilometers from each other. The first five sites were all places that were important in helping the slave trade, while the last two were buildings built in the early 1800s to stop the slave trade. Fort Bullen and the Six-Gun Battery are the only military buildings known to have been built to stop the slave trade.

In 2011, the island was renamed "Kunta Kinteh Island" from its original name of "James Island."

It is named after one of Gambia's most famous citizens, Kunta Kinteh, a man who was captured in Gambia and sold as a slave in America. The book and show *Roots*, which has become famous around the world, is based on Kunta Kinteh's life. Although seeing some of these sites may be painful, it is important to remember the role these buildings played in human history, and to make sure such terrible things never happen again.

Memphis and Its Necropolis—the Pyramid Fields from Giza to Dahshur, Egypt
Cultural World Heritage Site since 1979

Who hasn't heard of the pyramids of Giza? This famous World Heritage Site in Egypt holds some of the best and largest relics from ancient Egypt. Surviving for 5,000 years, the pyramids, temples, statues, treasures, and artwork of the ancient Egyptian kings and the world they ruled are preserved at this site.

According to legend, an ancient king named Menes founded Memphis, the capital of ancient

Egypt, around 3000 BC. Menes is said to have been the first pharaoh to unite southern and northern Egypt, but

some historians believe Menes was not a real king.

Memphis was located at a strategic point at the mouth of the Nile River, which made the city a great place of trade, business, and culture in the ancient world. The ruins of Memphis not only include statues of ancient Egyptian gods and kings, including Ramses and Ramses II, but also the temple of Huta-Ka-Ptah. This famous temple was devoted to Ptah, the god of creation.

Just northwest of Memphis stands the step pyramid of Pharaoh Djoser, the first pyramid in Egyptian history. The structure was built around 2600 BC and has six levels, which look like steps from the sides. It is part of a huge burial ground that includes many courtyards and tombs.

Nearby on the Giza Plateau rise the three pyramids known around the world as the Pyramids of Giza. These were built around 2500 BC, and each honors a different pharaoh. To the east of the pyramids sits the Great Sphinx, a truly enormous statue that has the body of a lion and the head of a man. The face is believed to be that of Pharaoh Khafra.

Mosi-oa-Tunya/Victoria Falls National Park, Zambia and Zimbabwe
Natural World Heritage Site since 1989

This incredible waterfall fed by the Zambezi River is the world's "largest sheet of falling water." Measuring 1,708 meters across and 108 meters high, the waterfall is not the highest or widest waterfall in the world, but it is certainly the most impressive.

The waterfall is located on the border of Zambia and Zimbabwe. During February and March, when the Zambezi River is at its fullest, about 500 million liters of water fall per second. During the dry season, around November, this number drops to about 10 million liters per second. But no matter what the season, the waterfall

creates a beautiful cloud of mist that can be seen from over 20 kilometers away. The wetness from the mist supports an ecosystem that is similar to a rain forest near the falls. The constant mist also creates a frequent show of beautiful rainbows. During the full moon, "moonbows" can be seen in the mist of the waterfall.

In 1855, the famous Scottish explorer David Livingstone became the first white man to see the waterfall. He named it "Victoria Falls" in honor of the queen of England at the time, Queen Victoria. However, local people have been calling the waterfall "Mosi-oa-Tunya" for thousands of years. In the language of the Kololo people, it means "the smoke that thunders." This name is still in use today in Zambia.

Serengeti National Park, Tanzania
Natural World Heritage Site since 1981

Covering over 15,000 square kilometers of grassland, Serengeti National Park is home to some of the most amazing natural life and natural events in the world. Every year, hundreds of thousands of animals in the national park—zebras, wildebeests, antelopes, gazelles, and the animals that hunt them—travel in herds across the vast plains searching for water. It is one of the largest and most impressive natural migrations in the world.

The word "Serengeti" comes from the Maasai people, who have herded their animals on these African grasses for thousands of years. They called their land the "Siringitu," or "the place where the land moves on forever."

Serengeti National Park is at the center of the larger Serengeti ecosystem, which is home to many nature parks and animal sanctuaries. Because the basic features of the weather, plants, and some animals have not changed in this region for millions of years, the Serengeti is also considered one of the oldest ecosystems on earth. The national park is home to at least four endangered species: the black rhinoceros, cheetah, elephant, and wild dog.

Timbuktu, Mali
Cultural World Heritage Site since 1988

In the English language, the name Timbuktu has come to mean "a far-away land." It is a city that calls to mind busy marketplaces, clever merchants, and long lines of camels carrying the riches of Africa. In reality, Timbuktu is a city in Mali that sits on the southern edge of the Sahara Desert. But the history of Timbuktu is very rich, giving rise to many legends and stories about the once-great city.

Timbuktu originally started in the 5th century BC as a camp for the nomadic Tuareg people. The camp was guarded by an old woman named Buktu. As the city grew and became more settled, it became known as "Tim-Buktu," or "place of Buktu."

Timbuktu reached its peak in cultural, economic, and religious importance during the rule of Askia the Great, an emperor of the Songhai Empire (one of the largest Islamic empires during the 15th and 16th centuries). By then, Timbuktu had established the University of Sankore and was home to many other schools of Islamic learning. The city also had many mosques that helped to spread Islam throughout Africa. Timbuktu became a center for book-making and book-selling in Africa. Some of the books that survive today are considered cultural treasures for their beauty and for the record of African history that they contain.

But Timbuktu was also important for economic reasons. It was a necessary stop on many trade routes. Merchants carrying salt, gold, grain, ivory, books, and even slaves traveled to Timbuktu to sell their goods in the city's busy markets. Traders and businessmen of the Mediterranean knew that the only way they could get the riches of Africa was through Timbuktu.

The traditional city squares, mosques, and tombs of the ancient city represent the traditional building style of West Africa. These buildings can still be seen in Timbuktu; however, this World Heritage Site is considered threatened by modern development and desertification.

ASIA

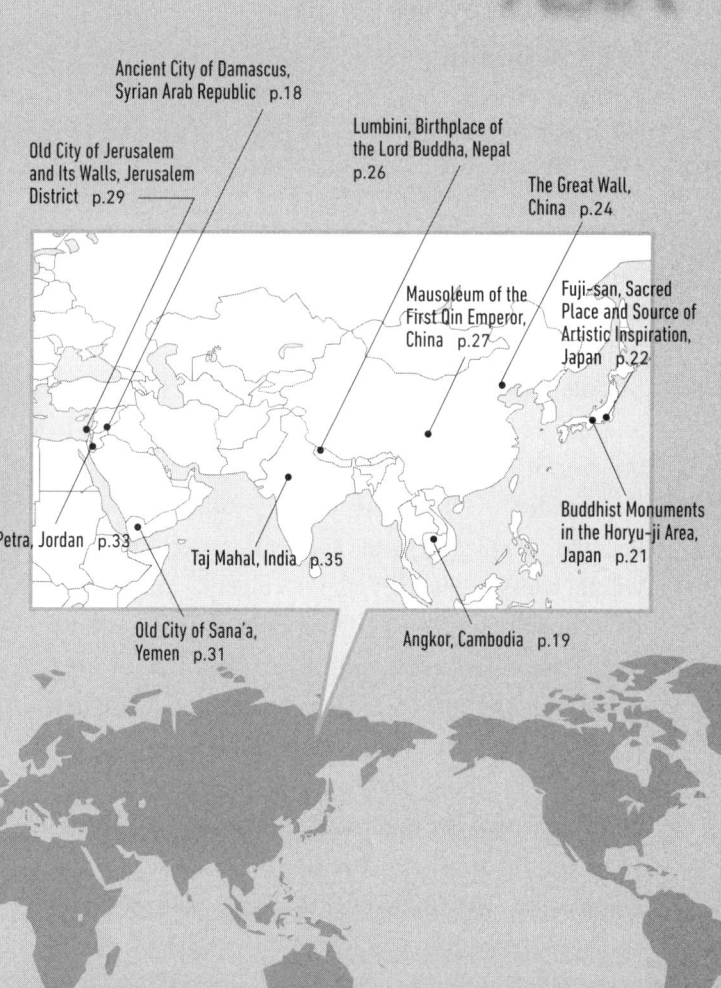

Ancient City of Damascus, Syrian Arab Republic p.18

Old City of Jerusalem and Its Walls, Jerusalem District p.29

Lumbini, Birthplace of the Lord Buddha, Nepal p.26

The Great Wall, China p.24

Mausoleum of the First Qin Emperor, China p.27

Fuji-san, Sacred Place and Source of Artistic Inspiration, Japan p.22

Petra, Jordan p.33

Buddhist Monuments in the Horyu-ji Area, Japan p.21

Taj Mahal, India p.35

Old City of Sana'a, Yemen p.31

Angkor, Cambodia p.19

Ancient City of Damascus, Syrian Arab Republic

Cultural World Heritage Site since 1979 (In Danger)

Damascus, often mentioned in stories of the ancient Middle East, is a truly one-of-a-kind city. People have continued to live in Damascus for about 2,400 years, making it one of the oldest cities in the Middle East, one of the oldest capitals in the world, and one of the oldest continually inhabited cities in the world.

Founded in the 3rd century BC, Damascus became a cultural and economic meeting place where the Orient met the Occident, and where Africa came into contact with Asia. Although there is evidence that people may have inhabited the area of Damascus since as early as 8,000 BC, it became a world-class city during the Middle Ages. Some early civilizations, such as that of the Arameans and Assyrians, got their start in Damascus. As time went on, civilizations rose and fell in and around Damascus. The influence of many empires and cultures can be seen in Damascus, including Greek, Roman, Islamic, and Byzantine cultures.

Damascus is home to one of the largest mosques in the world. Muslims have continued to pray at the Umayyad Great Mosque, also known as the Grand Mosque of Damascus, for roughly 1,300 years.

Today, Damascus is considered a World Heritage Site in Danger. Due to the harm caused by the Syrian civil war, all six World Heritage Sites in Syria have been put on the "In Danger" list. Sadly, some incredible cultural sites and treasures have already been destroyed by the war.

Angkor, Cambodia
Cultural World Heritage Site since 1992

The vast ruins of Angkor serves as evidence of the grandness of the ancient Khmer Kingdom. From roughly the 9th to 15th centuries, the Khmer made up the strongest empire in Southeast Asia. Angkor was the site for several capital cities, with different kings adding buildings, temples, and other structures to the area as time went on.

Located just 6 kilometers south of Siem Reap

in present-day Cambodia, the ruins of Angkor are protected today as the Angkor Archaeological Park. Angkor covers over 400 square kilometers of land and contains the largest ancient city in the world. The ruins are an incredible sight to see.

Some of the most striking features of Angkor are its temples, which are full of symbolism. The temples, including the famous Angkor Wat, are built to look like mountains to represent Mount Meru, which Hindus believe is the center of the universe. Mount Meru has five high points, and so too do many of the temples at Angkor. However, the city of Angkor had both Hindu and Buddhist rulers, so the architecture of the city changed back and forth, representing Hindu values and Buddhist values.

The most impressive Buddhist temple at Angkor is the Bayon, which was built by the Buddhist king Jayavarman VII around the late 12th century. Al-

though different rulers have changed or added to the temple over time, today the most striking feature of the Bayon are the huge stone faces carved into the temple's towers. These faces are said to represent the bodhisattva Avalokitasvara, but many people say the faces also look very much like Jayavarman VII.

Buddhist Monuments in the Horyu-ji Area, Japan
Cultural World Heritage Site since 1993

The Buddhist temple grounds of Horyu-ji is one of Japan's best-loved cultural and historical sites. Located in Ikaruga in Nara Prefecture, Horyu-ji is home to some of the oldest wooden buildings in the world. There are many legends, stories, songs, and poems that honor Horyu-ji, and the national government has declared the site one of Japan's National Treasures.

The history of Horyu-ji is carved onto the back of a statue of the Yakushi Nyorai Buddha in the temple's Golden Hall or Pavilion. As the story goes, Emperor Yomei, who was the 31st emperor of Japan, fell very ill. As a form of prayer and a way to cure his illness, Yomei promised to build a Buddhist temple. However, he died from his illness before he was able to fulfill this promise. After several years, Yomei's sister, Suiko, became empress. Together with her nephew Prince Shotoku, who was deeply Buddhist, Empress Suiko built Horyu-ji and fulfilled Yomei's wish.

The temple was completed in 607 AD. Today, the grounds of the World Heritage Site include 48 Buddhist structures, of which 28 were built in or before the 8th century. These buildings are considered the earliest Buddhist structures in Japan. The buildings also represent important cultural and artistic advances in Japan because they are based on Chinese architecture but show the evolution of Japanese style and design.

Fuji-san, Sacred Place and Source of Artistic Inspiration, Japan
Cultural World Heritage Site since 2013

Although Mount Fuji has long been an important source of Japanese national pride, this legendary mountain is one of the newest World Heritage Sites. Along with 18 other sites around the world,

UNESCO officially recognized Fuji-san as a World Heritage Site in 2013, making the holy mountain Japan's 17th World Heritage Site.

Mount Fuji is a volcanic mountain that rises 3,776 meters. Located about 100 kilometers southwest of Tokyo, it has captured the minds and imaginations of poets, artists, writers, and other creative people for centuries. Fuji-san is also considered a religious site, and thousands of Buddhist and Shinto worshippers travel to the mountain every year to pay respects to this holy site.

Artistic representations of Fuji-san that still exist today date back to 11th century. Also, from the 14th century on, Japanese artists made many wood-block prints of Fuji-san. These were made popular around the world, especially the works of the famous print maker, Katsushika Hokusai. These images even influenced many Western Impressionist artists such as Edgar Degas, Paul Gauguin, Claude Monet, Pierre-Auguste Renoir, and Vincent van Gogh.

The recognized World Heritage Site includes 25 different spots that represent the artistic, cultural, and spiritual value of Fuji-san. These areas include the mountain itself, Lake Yamanaka, Lake Kawaguchi, Fujisan Hongu Sengen Taisha, eight Oshino Hakkai hot springs, and Shiraito Falls, among others.

The Great Wall, China
Cultural World Heritage Site since 1987

What makes the Great Wall of China so great? For a while, some people believed the wall was so great in size that it could even be seen from the moon. This has been proven not to be true, but that does not make this historical structure any less great.

Military walls for protection against warring groups began to be built in China as early as the 7th century BC. Some of these were built for Chinese lords to protect their kingdoms from each other. For example, in 408 BC the Wei built a wall to protect their land against the Qin forces. Then in the 3rd century BC, the first emperor of China, Qin Shi Huang, made various walls bigger and joined some of them together to protect the southern kingdoms from northern invaders. From this point on, the wall continued to grow until the 17th century. Building, fixing, and improving the wall became something of a military tradition in China.

However, it was the Ming Dynasty (1368–1644) that did the most work on the Great Wall. During this time, 5,650 kilometers of wall was built. The wall's purpose was not only to protect China from the foreign forces that surrounded it, but also to preserve China's culture from outside influences.

Today, the Great Wall is an important part of Chinese history, literature, and culture. It is over 20,000 kilometers long. It starts at the Hushan Great Wall in Liaoning Province in the east and ends at Jiayuguan City in Gansu Province in the west. Every year, the wall attracts over 4 million visitors.

Lumbini, Birthplace of the Lord Buddha, Nepal
Cultural World Heritage Site since 1997

Lumbini, just south of the Himalaya Mountains in the Terai Plains of Nepal, is recognized as the place where Siddhartha Gautama, the Lord Buddha, was born. It is believed that the Buddha was born between 623 and 543 BC. Soon after the Buddha's death, Lumbini became famous around the world, and the site has drawn visits from millions of Buddhists throughout history. According to recent figures, Lumbini draws an average of 400,000 visitors every year.

Lumbini is one of the holiest places of the Buddhist religion. When the Buddha was alive, the area was a beautiful garden full of trees. The Bud-

dha's father was King Suddhodana, a warrior and a member of the Shakya family. His mother, Queen Maya Devi, gave birth to the Buddha on her way to her parents' house in

Devadaha. As she rested under a tree in the gardens of Lumbini, the Buddha was born.

According to ancient writings, the Buddha lived in Lumbini until he was 29 years old. After that, he traveled throughout the land, searching for enlightenment. Today, Lumbini is home to a number of temples, monuments to Buddha, and ruins from ancient times. The Indian Emperor Ashoka came to Lumbini in 249 BC to visit the holy site of Buddha's birth. Once there, he built four stupas (Buddhist monuments) to honor the Buddha.

In 1996, archaeologists dug up a beautiful, old stone in Lumbini. It is believed that in 249 BC, King Ashoka placed a stone at the exact site of the Buddha's birth. Further study may prove that this was the stone that Ashoka placed there so long ago.

Mausoleum of the First Qin Emperor, China
Cultural World Heritage Site since 1987

One of China's most fascinating historical sites was discovered completely by accident. In 1974, a group of farmers digging a well in Xi'an, Shaanxi Province, came across a strange site. Below the earth were artistic pieces of terracotta pottery—statues, in fact—and they appeared to be very, very old. When news of this spread around the region, it attracted the attention of a team of Chinese archaeologists. The team immediately traveled to Xi'an to discover one of the greatest archaeological finds of the 20th century.

The farmers had accidentally found the underground tomb of Qin Shi Huang, the first emperor of China, who lived in the 3rd century BC. The 2,200-year-old statue they had come across turned out to be part of an entire clay army buried underground. There were soldiers of various ranks, generals, horses, and even war chariots. There were over 8,000 terracotta soldiers in the underground army.

According to historical records, Qin Shi Huang began construction of his mausoleum as soon as he became the king of Qin at 13 years old. He chose a location at the foot of Mount Li. It is believed that 700,000 workers from all over China worked on the mausoleum, and they continued to work as Qin Shi Huang won battle after battle. He unified much of

China, became emperor, and ruled for about 10 years before his death. By the time he was buried, the mausoleum had been turned into a clay model of the emperor's palace and the city surrounding it, protected by a life-sized army.

The emperor was also buried with statues of entertainers and musicians, as well as jewels and treasures. These were protected with weapons that were built to shoot possible thieves. The clothes, hair styles, and faces of the statues are incredibly detailed and reveal the styles of the time period. Archaeologists continue to dig at the site today. A museum has been built at the site, and it attracts more than a million visitors per year.

Old City of Jerusalem and Its Walls, Jerusalem District
Cultural World Heritage Site since 1981 (In Danger)

Recognized as a holy site by three world religions—Christianity, Islam, and Judaism—the Old City of

Jerusalem is very important to billions of people around the world. Because the city was located in a strategic position on the Mediterranean Sea near the Judean Mountains, many societies and kingdoms fought to control it. The city and its walls were repeatedly destroyed and rebuilt for centuries.

The city contains 220 historic monuments that cover hundreds, sometimes thousands, of years of history. Sadly, in 1982, this ancient, culturally important city was officially declared by UNESCO to be in danger because of civil conflict and war in the area.

The Old City is a small district located within the modern city of Jerusalem. It is surrounded by an ancient wall that is packed with history: according to the Bible, Jerusalem was surrounded by a strong, protective wall even before King David took over the city in the 11th century BC. His son, King Solomon, extended the walls, and many centuries later, in about 440 BC, the walls were rebuilt. In roughly 41 AD, Herod Agrippa, a Jewish King who was in power at the time, built a new city wall. After this long Jewish and Christian history, the city became a major center of Islam during the 7th century.

However, Jerusalem changed over the ages, and the Old City gained new buildings and landmarks as fast as old ones were destroyed. The current city walls were built by the Ottoman Empire in 1538. Inside the city walls is an amazing variety of churches, temples, mosques, and other cultural buildings and sights such as the Dome of the Rock, the Wailing Wall, and the Church of the Holy Sepulchre.

The city is divided into four quarters. These are the Muslim Quarter, Jewish Quarter, Christian Quarter, and Armenian Quarter. It is truly a melting pot of cultural influence, but sadly, many residents of Jerusalem and the surrounding area have not been able to put aside their cultural differences. To this day, cultural and religious fighting continues in the area.

Old City of Sana'a, Yemen
Cultural World Heritage Site since 1986

Located high up in a mountain valley in Yemen, the Old City of Sana'a has witnessed roughly 2,500 years of human life and activity. It has been an important trading post throughout history. It became the capital city of Yemen in 1962, and it continues to be an important historical, cultural, and economic center of the Middle East today.

Although there is evidence that people have lived in the area of Sana'a since roughly 2,500 years ago, the city of Sana'a was officially founded in the 2nd century BC. Back then, it was just a border town on the edge of the Yemenite kingdoms. But during the 1st century AD, it became an important stop on several trade routes.

In the 7th century, Sana'a became a world center for Islamic culture and teachings. The city's Great Mosque is said to have been built while the Prophet Muhammad was still alive. Sana'a helped to spread Islam throughout the world, and the city began

to reflect traditional Islamic art, design, and architecture. To this day, the ancient city is filled with beautiful, tall, red-and-white buildings built of packed earth and brick. Minarets reach for the sky, and the tower-like houses are decorated in a traditional Islamic style.

Sana'a is still a very active city, as it is home to a population of almost two million people. It is perhaps one of the most unique cities in the world.

Petra, Jordan
Cultural World Heritage Site since 1985

Petra is one of the world's most famous and best-loved archaeological sites. Its name, Petra, means "rock" in Greek. This is because much of the ancient city is made out of stone. Its beautiful temples and public buildings are in fact carved out of the red, rocky mountains and cliffs that surround the city. Many of these mountains hold an incredible network of man-made tunnels and paths. Petra also became a part of popular culture when scenes from the movie *Indiana Jones and the Last Crusade* were filmed there.

Petra is located between the Red Sea and Dead Sea in present-day Jordan. Archaeologists say that people have lived in Petra since prehistoric times. The city became the capital of the Nabatean people around the 4th century BC, when the region was a very important stopping point for people traveling over several trade routes. Merchants trading Chinese silk, Indian spices, or Arabian spices would pass through Petra on their way to foreign markets. Throughout history, Petra also came under the rule of many great empires, including the Egyptians, Greeks, and Romans. The influences of many cultures made their mark on Petra, making it a crossroads for Eastern, Western, and African culture.

Although this region of Jordan is very dry, the citizens of Petra created amazing ways of tapping, catching, storing, and transporting water. Their water management system allowed the population of Petra to grow, despite the region's desert-like climate.

Petra is full of beautiful temples, churches, tombs, public buildings, and man-made networks that cut through the red cliffs. One of the most impressive structures at Petra is Al Khazneh, also known as

"The Treasury." Al Khazneh stands about 40 meters tall, is built in the Greek style, and is carved out of the red cliff face.

Archaeologists have dug up only about 15 percent of the city, but many historical and artistic treasures, such as ancient books, pottery, paintings, and coins, have been found.

Taj Mahal, India
Cultural World Heritage Site since 1983

Perhaps one of the most famous buildings in the world, the Taj Mahal, has a touching love story behind it. Shah Jahan, a Mughal emperor who lived in the 17th century, loved his third wife very deeply. He called her "Mumtaz Mahal," or "Chosen One of the Palace," because she was his favorite of all the women he knew. According to legend, Mumtaz Mahal was so beautiful that even the moon could not compare to her beauty.

Mumtaz Mahal died during child labor. But, as the story goes, before she died, she made Shah Jahan promise to build her the most beautiful tomb that anyone had ever seen. Whether or not this is true, the emperor was truly heartbroken over her death. He hired 20,000 workers who came from all over India and Central Asia to build a monument to his wife. More than 15 years later, the workers completed the Taj Mahal, which means "the crown of palaces." Mumtaz Mahal was buried here, and years later, Shah Jahan was buried next to her.

The Taj Mahal is located on the shore of the Yamuna River in the city of Agra in the state of Uttar Pradesh in India. The Taj Mahal is made of white marble. The octagon-shaped tomb is the focus of the whole structure. The walls of the tomb are richly decorated with Islamic calligraphy and jewels. Surrounding the tomb are four minarets, and the grounds include vast gardens, a part of the Yamuna River, a mosque, living quarters, and a marketplace. About 7 million people visit the Taj Mahal every year.

AUSTRALIA & OCEANIA

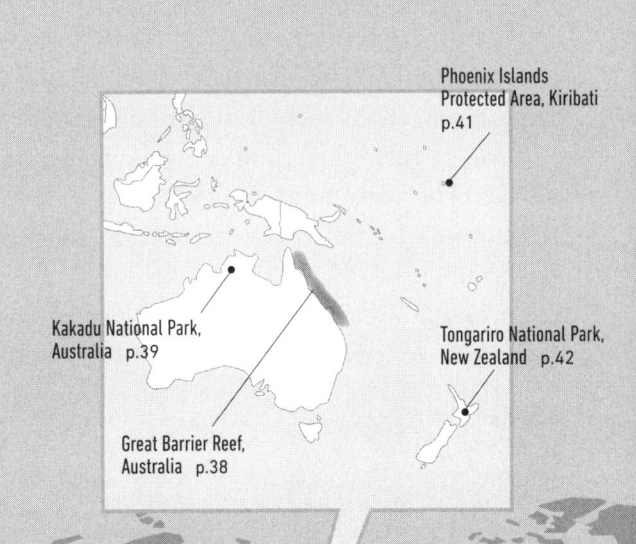

Phoenix Islands Protected Area, Kiribati p.41

Kakadu National Park, Australia p.39

Tongariro National Park, New Zealand p.42

Great Barrier Reef, Australia p.38

Great Barrier Reef, Australia
Natural World Heritage Site since 1981

Did you know the Great Barrier Reef is the biggest structure on Earth built by living things? But the living things responsible for building it are tiny—some no bigger than a centimeter. Over 50 million years, countless coral polyps created the Great Barrier Reef by simply going through their natural life cycle.

Coral polyps are related to sea anemones and jellyfish. They have soft bodies with a hard skeleton on the bottom. They live by attaching to a rock and capturing pieces of plant matter floating in the sea and sometimes even tiny fish. Coral polyps divide themselves to create more coral polyps, and in this way, a colony forms. Coral reefs are created when these colonies die and the polyps leave behind their hard skeletons. It is a very slow process, as reefs only grow about 1.3 centimeters per year. The Great Barrier Reef was created by hundreds of different colonies in the ocean growing large enough to connect to each other.

Located just northeast off the coast of Australia and stretching about 2,000 kilometers north to south, the Great Barrier Reef covers an area of about 350,000 square kilometers in total. It is one of the most biologically diverse places on Earth. It is home to over 2,000 species of fish, and new ones continue to be found. There are also more than 250 species of shrimp and more than 4,000 species of mollusks. Coral reefs also attract many types of plant life, fish, and even larger sea animals, such as dolphins and turtles. Because of this, the Great Barrier Reef is a truly special and beautiful natural site.

Kakadu National Park, Australia
Cultural and Natural World Heritage Site since 1981

Kakadu National Park in Australia is so special because of the amount of prehistoric cultural information and history it reveals. People have been living in the area for more than 40,000 years and continue to do so today.

Aside from the wonderful natural features of the park, such as its lakes, meadows, forests, mountains, cliffs, and vast number of species of plant and animal life, the area is also home to cultural treasures of the Aboriginal Australian people, such as ancient rock paintings and archaeological findings. Many of the rock paintings are thousands of years old. More than 5,000 artistic and cultural sites exist in the park.

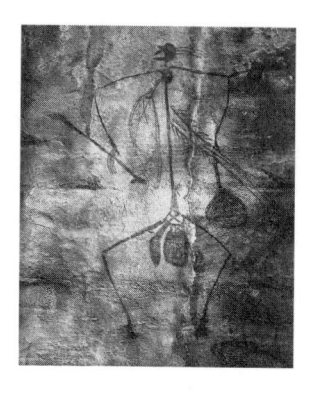

Until very recently, the Aboriginal peoples who live in Kakadu today continued much of the same hunting-and-gathering lifestyles that their ancestors practiced thousands of years ago. Today, these hunting practices are rare, but the customs and beliefs of the Aboriginal people are still tied to the traditions that have survived for thousands of years. In this way, the park holds human, living evidence as well as archaeological evidence of over thousands of years of history.

Kakadu also holds incredible natural value for the various ecosystems and species that exist

AUSTRALIA & OCEANIA

within the 20,000-square-kilometer stretch of land. Kakadu holds some of the richest variety of plants and animals found in Australia, with over 10,000 insect species, 1,600 plant species, 280 bird species, and 60 mammal species.

Phoenix Islands Protected Area, Kiribati
Natural World Heritage Site since 2010

The Republic of Kiribati is a group of 33 islands in the middle of the Pacific Ocean between Australia and Hawaii. Eight of these islands are known as the Phoenix Islands, and since 2010 they have been recognized as a World Heritage Site for the natural wonders they hold. The protected area covers an area of 408,250 square kilometers, including both land and ocean. This makes the Phoenix Islands Protected Area the largest World Heritage Site in the world.

Humans live on only one Phoenix Island. They are sent there by the government of Kiribati to help care for the area. The natural treasures found at and around the Phoenix Islands include underwater volcanoes and mountains, coral reefs, 500 species of fish, 200 species of coral, 44 bird species, and 18 sea mammals. Some animals that are now very rare in other parts of the world are still common in the Phoenix Islands Protected Area. Humans have had very little contact and influence on the reefs and islands here, making the ocean ecosystems some of the best and healthiest in the world.

For the Phoenix Islands to continue being the pure, natural treasure that it is, the area is heavily protected from human threats such as over-fishing and development.

Tongariro National Park, New Zealand
Cultural and Natural World Heritage Site since 1993

The oldest national park in New Zealand and the fourth established national park in the world, Tongariro is recognized by UNESCO for having both cultural and natural value. The high, snow-capped mountains that rise in the middle of the park hold deep spiritual meaning for the Maori people, who are native to New Zealand. In addition, the park is home to three active volcanoes, Mount Ruapehu, Mount Ngauruhoe, and Mount Tongariro. There are also lava, ice fields, and glaciers in the park. The park covers roughly 800 square kilometers of land on the northern island of New Zealand.

It is believed that the Maori arrived in the nation known today as New Zealand possibly as early as AD 600. They carried plants and animals from their former Polynesian villages to the new islands, which they called "Aotearoa." Once they arrived, they created a rich, unique culture. The mountains and volcanoes of Tongariro were at the center of some of this culture's arts, beliefs, and customs.

In the late 1800s, the mountains were in danger of being sold to European settlers who were arriving in greater numbers in New Zealand. Because the Maori loved their mountains so much, they came up with a plan to save them. Instead of selling them off, the local Maori gave the land surrounding the mountains to the British queen. However, they would only give their precious mountains as a gift on one condition: that the land would be protected as a national park. The queen promised to keep the Maori's one condition. The land then became Tongariro National Park, and the mountains and their natural setting continue to be protected to this day.

EUROPE

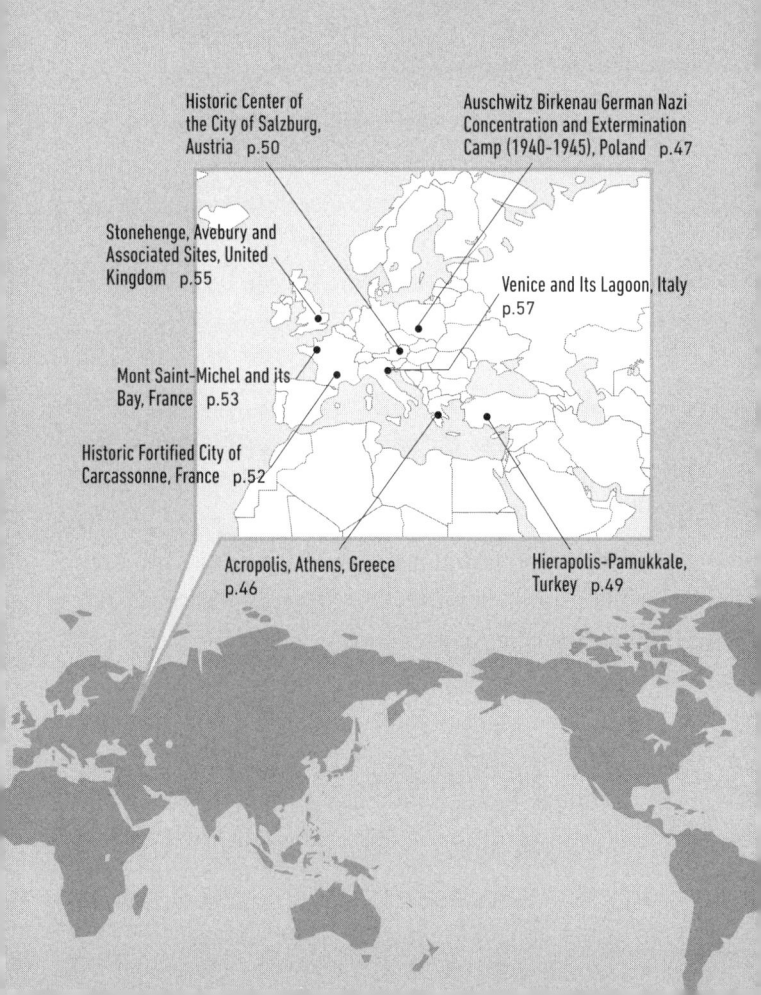

Historic Center of the City of Salzburg, Austria p.50

Auschwitz Birkenau German Nazi Concentration and Extermination Camp (1940-1945), Poland p.47

Stonehenge, Avebury and Associated Sites, United Kingdom p.55

Venice and Its Lagoon, Italy p.57

Mont Saint-Michel and its Bay, France p.53

Historic Fortified City of Carcassonne, France p.52

Acropolis, Athens, Greece p.46

Hierapolis-Pamukkale, Turkey p.49

Acropolis, Athens, Greece

Cultural World Heritage Site since 1987

The ancient Greeks have been one of the most influential societies in the Western world. The Acropolis in Athens is a monument to Greek thought, design, and style. Seeing and understanding the Acropolis gives one a true appreciation for the early civilization that helped shape the culture of the West.

Standing on the top of a rocky hill, the Acropolis looks down on the city of Athens, the capital of Greece and one of the world's oldest cities. In Greek, the word acropolis means "upper city" or "high city." Many Greek settlements were planned this way for protection, including religious and military centers. Although all such settlements are considered acropolises, the Acropolis of Athens is Greece's most famous.

Although there is evidence that humans lived on the hill above Athens as early as 5,000 years ago, the most important buildings visible at the Acropolis today were built in the 5th century BC by Pericles, an excellent general and leader of Athens. These buildings include the Propylaea (the main gate to the Acropolis), the Parthenon (the temple of the goddess Athena), the Erechtheion (a temple dedicated to both Athena and Poseidon, the god of the sea), and the Temple of Athena Nike (another temple to Athena).

Over time, the Acropolis came to be used and influenced by different societies in power, including the Byzantines, the Turks, and the Franks. Many treasures have been taken from the Acropolis through the centuries, but today, it is undergoing some of the most advanced conservation efforts in the world. It is certainly one of the best-loved historical sites in the world.

Auschwitz Birkenau German Nazi Concentration and Extermination Camp (1940-1945), Poland
Cultural World Heritage Site since 1979

Auschwitz Birkenau, the most famous of the six German Nazi concentration camps, is now a symbol of the worst of humanity. The ways in which people were treated in Auschwitz is so unbelievable that the evidence has been protected as a World Heritage Site to remember one of the saddest events in modern history. Today, the former concentration camp reminds visitors of the terrors of institutionalized hate.

When Soviet soldiers took over Auschwitz at the end of World War II, they could not believe what they saw inside. It was worse than a prison—it was a place of extreme cruelty, slave labor, and mass murder. Thousands of people, starved and sick, lived in terrible, unclean conditions. They were only kept alive to work as slaves, and when workers became too sick to be useful, they were killed. Every day, hundreds of Jews and other non-Aryan people were shipped into Auschwitz on trains and were sent to gas chambers to die.

Auschwitz was the largest of the Nazi concentration camps. It consisted of three main camps—a base camp, an extermination camp, and a labor camp—as well as 45 smaller camps surrounding the area. It employed about 7,000 Nazis. In total, over a million people were held and murdered at this camp. About 90 percent of them were Jews. It is estimated that one in six Jews who died during the Holocaust died at Auschwitz.

Hierapolis-Pamukkale, Turkey
Cultural and Natural World Heritage Site since 1988

Hierapolis-Pamukkale is one of the 29 recognized World Heritage Sites (as of the year 2013) with "mixed" cultural and natural value. It is one of the most unique hot springs in the world, and the site plays an interesting role in Turkish history.

In Turkish, the word Pammukale means "cotton castle." The ancient Turks called the site this because of its unique, white landscape. The hot springs that come up in that particular area carry large amounts of calcite, a white mineral. After thousands of years, the calcite built up to create an incredible white landscape of pools, terraces, and natural formations that looked like frozen forests.

The temperature of the hot springs is a pleasant 35 degrees Celsius. The ancient people living around the area found the warm waters to have healing powers. They built a city, Hierapolis, at the site in the 2nd century BC, which the Romans took over in 129 BC. The ruins of Hierapolis include buildings and public works influenced by a number of societies—the Greek, the Byzantines, the Romans, the Jews, and the Anatolians. Some of the major buildings include public baths, a theater, a large cemetery, churches and temples, such as the Temple of Apollo, and other monuments. The site has international value both as a natural wonder and as an important piece of Turkish history.

....

Historic Center of the City of Salzburg, Austria
Cultural World Heritage Site since 1996

The home of Wolfgang Amadeus Mozart is well known not only for its musical culture and history, but also for its architectural beauty. Surrounded by mountains and caught between Germany and Italy, the city displays a unique blend of German and Italian thought, art, and influences.

For a long time, Salzburg was a religious city-state, ruled by a prince who was also a bishop. Because of this, much of Salzburg is devoted to religion: it has a vast number of churches, cathedrals, monasteries, and religious monuments. Some of its most famous buildings are the Franciscan Abbey, the Benedictine Abbey of Saint Peter, and the cathedral of Saint Rupert and Saint Virgil.

Salzburg is one of the few cities in the world to have held onto its role as a religious city-state into the 19th century. Because of this, the city has important historical and political value as well.

Although most of the buildings in Salzburg reflect the Baroque period, many of the city's treasures are much older. The Abbey of Saint Peter, for example, was founded in the 7th century, while the Nonnberg Benedictine Nunnery is considered the oldest nunnery north of the Alps. Today, Salzburg is the fourth-largest city in Austria. Some scenes from the movie *The Sound of Music* were filmed in Salzburg, and the city draws many visitors each year.

Historic Fortified City of Carcassonne, France

Cultural World Heritage Site since 1997

Today, Carcassonne is considered one of the world's finest examples of a medieval fortified town. With its huge protective walls, stone castle, tall towers, and Gothic cathedral, Carcassonne looks very much like a town from a fairy tale.

Carcassonne is built on a hill in southern France. Archaeologists believe that people have lived on the hill since 3500 BC, and a prehistoric fort stood on the same hill as early as the 6th century BC. The hill has always been the perfect place for a fort, looking over the early trade routes that connected the Atlantic Sea to the Mediterranean.

Although Carcassonne became part of the Roman Empire in the 1st century BC, it changed hands among many different European societies throughout history because of its desirable location. However, it always remained a strong city, difficult to attack and take over. In fact, Carcassonne was so strong that it was never attacked during the Hundred Years' War in the 1300 and 1400s.

During the mid-1800s, Carcassonne attracted the attention of a French architect and conservationist, Eugene-Emmanuel Viollet-le-Duc. He worked for many years to restore the fort at Carcassonne. Viollet-le-Duc was one of the first people to work in the field of restoration, and his work at Carcassonne influenced many others around the world.

Today, Carcassonne has made it into popular culture, with a board game and a video game named after it. Scenes from the movie *Robin Hood: Prince of Thieves* were filmed in and around Carcassonne. It draws millions of visitors a year.

Mont Saint-Michel and its Bay, France
Cultural World Heritage Site since 1979

Together with Italy and China, France is one of the top three countries in the world with the most World Heritage Sites. Thirty-eight World Heritage Sites can be found across France, but the abbey of Mont Saint-Michel is perhaps one of the most interesting and enchanting. Built on a tiny, rocky island just one kilometer from the Normandy coast, Mont Saint-Michel is one of France's most visited sites.

The island of Mont Saint-Michel is only 1 square kilometer in area. Currently, only 44 people live there. In ancient times, the island was an important military post, but during the 6th century, monks looking for a quiet life of solitude started to live there.

In the 8th century, a monastery was built on the island. Over the centuries, a little village grew around the monastery. Although the island and its monastery has been used for different purposes throughout history—during the 14th century as a military post, and during the 19th century as a prison—monks have always returned to the island. And ever since the abbey was built, Mont Saint-Michel has been one of the most popular religious sites for Christian pilgrims to visit.

In medieval times, people could only get to Mont Saint-Michel when the water level in the bay was very low. Travelers could then walk across the sand to the island. However, in the 1800s, a high road was built to connect the island to land, so people could visit at any time.

Stonehenge, Avebury and Associated Sites, United Kingdom
Cultural World Heritage Site since 1986

Great Britain is home to the prehistoric stone monuments at Stonehenge and Avebury in Wiltshire County. For ages, people wondered who built these huge stone circles and how. Today, we have some answers to these mysteries.

The two ancient monuments are roughly 50 kilometers apart from each other, with Avebury to the north and Stonehenge to the south. Avebury holds the largest prehistoric stone circle in the world, while Stonehenge holds the most well-designed prehistoric stone circle in the world.

Scientists, historians, and archaeologists worked together to figure out that several different groups of prehistoric people built or worked on Stonehenge in different stages, or periods of time. The first stage happened around 3000 BC, when early peoples dug a huge trench using deer antlers and bones. Over the next 200 years, the circle was improved with wooden posts. Then stones were added over centuries, starting at around 2500 BC. Then the final touch—the huge stones that support a cross-piece overhead, were added around 2000 BC. Some of these stones were transported from 240 kilometers away, and the largest of these stones weighs about 36,280 kilograms.

It is believed that Stonehenge was built by three different groups of people over time—first the Windmill Hill People (who came from eastern England), then the Beaker People (who are thought to have come from Spain), and finally the Wessex People (related to the prehistoric people of France).

The World Heritage Site includes other prehistoric monuments grouped close by the two stone circles, including the Cursus, the Avenue, Durrington Walls, and Woodhenge at the Stonehenge site. At Avebury, the recognized sites include the West Kennet Long Barrow, the Sanctuary, and Silbury Hill. Both monuments at Stonehenge and Avebury seem to line up with the sun's seasonal path in the sky, but what this means is still a mystery.

Venice and Its Lagoon, Italy
Cultural World Heritage Site since 1987

The name Venice brings to mind charming canals, gondolas, narrow streets, grand plazas, and famous Italian artists. It is perhaps one of the most romantic cities in the world, and for good reason. The city of Venice has long been considered one of the finest examples of Italian architecture and art.

Venice is built on 118 small islands in Laguna Veneta (or Venetian Lagoon), off of the Adriatic Sea. The city is named after the Veneti people who are thought to have lived in the region as early as the 10th century BC.

Founded in the 5th century, Venice started as a humble collection of camps set up by people escaping attacks from northern Germanic groups. However, the camps slowly became established villages, and finally, these villages combined and turned into a large city. Because of its location near major trading routes and other ports, Venice became an important center for international trade and business.

Between the 9th to the 12th centuries, Venice developed into a city-state. Its citizens were known around the Mediterranean as excellent sailors. The Venetians, who had grown rich from centuries of trade and business overseas, began to spend their extra money on art. This drew many artists to Venice, and the city became famous for its high-quality arts and crafts.

Today, Venice is better known for its Carnival culture, its romantic canals, its beautiful buildings, and the great works of art that can be found in almost every church and public building in the city. But in the 20th century, the city started sinking, and floods became a frequent threat. However, this does not stop Venice from being one of the most popular tourist destinations in the world. Today Venice draws visits from almost 3 million people per year.

NORTH & CENTRAL AMERICA

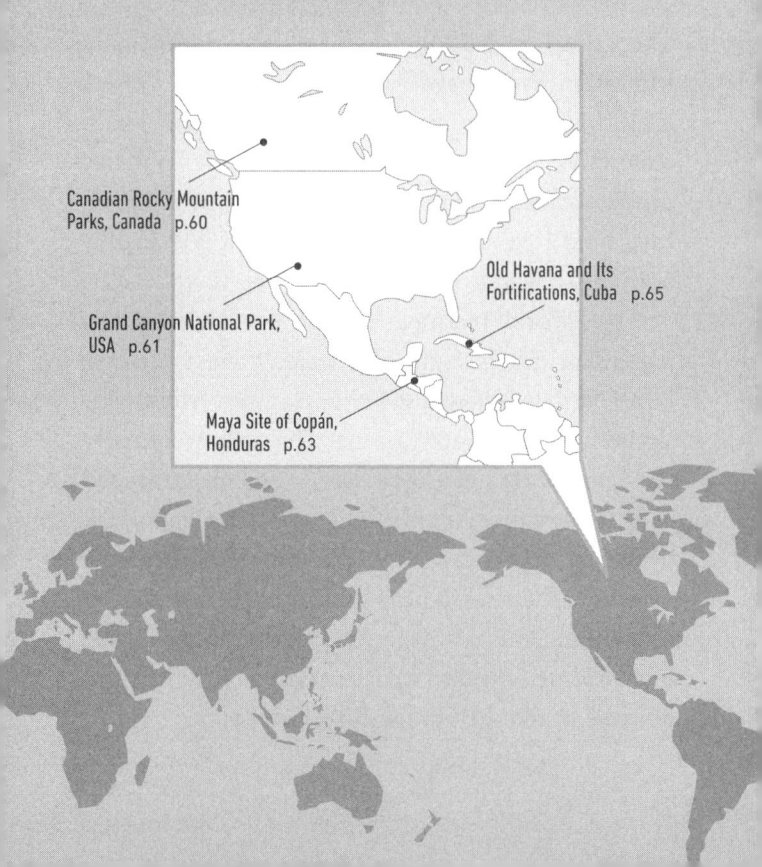

Canadian Rocky Mountain Parks, Canada p.60

Grand Canyon National Park, USA p.61

Old Havana and Its Fortifications, Cuba p.65

Maya Site of Copán, Honduras p.63

Canadian Rocky Mountain Parks, Canada
Natural World Heritage Site since 1990

The Canadian Rocky Mountain Parks have it all: soaring mountains, glaciers, clear blue lakes, waterfalls, thick forests, ice fields, cave systems, canyons, hot springs, and alpine meadows. It is a vast, wild area of natural beauty, which is visited by millions of people every year.

This World Heritage Site covers seven nature parks, including some of Canada's most famous: Banff, Jasper, Kootenay, Yoho, Hamber, Mount Assiniboine, and Mount Robson. The site also includes the famous Burgess Shale site, which is estimated to be 505 million years old. It is such an important historical and natural site because it is one of the world's earliest fossil beds that contain the fossils of soft-bodied animals. It has been incredibly valuable in providing scientists with evidence of the evolution of some of the earliest life forms on Earth.

The Canadian Rocky Mountains stretch for roughly 1,450 kilometers in a northwest to southeast direction. They are about 150 kilometers wide, and they lie across the Continental Divide of North America. The mountains are all limestone and shale, and the highest point is Mount Robson, which rises 3,954 meters. The glaciers and ice fields in the parks are still active, continuing the natural processes that have been forming North American landscapes for billions of years.

Grand Canyon National Park, USA
Natural World Heritage Site since 1979

Nearly 5 million people visit Grand Canyon National Park in the state of Arizona every year. One look at the canyon's size, colors, and shape reveals why this is such a popular destination: the Grand Canyon is one of the most incredible gorges in the world.

The cliffs of the Grand Canyon show over two billion years of history. The canyon cut by the Colorado River stretches for about 446 kilometers. At some places, the canyon is 29 kilometers wide and 1.6 kilometers deep. According to scientists, the Grand Canyon was formed over 17 million years of natural processes, and these processes continue today.

Evidence of all four major geological eras of the Earth can be found in the rock of the Grand Canyon: the early and late Precambrian, Palaeozoic, Mesozoic, and Cenozoic eras. Early plant and animal forms have been captured in the rock of the Grand Canyon, becoming fossils. The area is also rich with cultural value because it was inhabited by prehistoric peoples as early as 8000 BC. Many actually lived within in the canyons, either using natural caves for shelter or carving homes into the rock. There are over 2,600 prehistoric ruins within the park, all of which give clues as to how early Americans lived. Today, the area continues to be home to many Native Americans.

Maya Site of Copán, Honduras
Cultural World Heritage Site since 1980

The Mayan civilization was one of the most advanced and influential ancient cultures in the Americas. It is known today as the only culture to have had a fully developed written language in the Americas before the arrival of Europeans. The Mayans also had advanced knowledge and practices in astronomy, math, architecture, and art. Today, millions of people speak languages related to Mayan, and some of the ancient culture's traditions, religion, and beliefs live on in Honduras, Belize, Guatemala, El Salvador, and Mexico.

The city of Copán was the capital of the southern area of the Mayan kingdom from the 5th to 9th centuries AD. Today, Copán is considered one of the most important Mayan sites in the world. Located in western Honduras near the border of Guatemala, Copán sits in a valley and once covered an area of about 250 square kilometers.

During the height of its power, Copán was occupied by at least 20,000 people. However, the city was abandoned in the early 10th century. It had long been an empty city by the time Spanish explorers came across the city in the 16th century.

Beautiful detail and bold designs make Mayan art, sculpture, and architecture striking. Copán's many stone temples, public buildings, statues, and other carved structures show that careful planning went into the creation of the city. Copán has five main areas that display great examples of Mayan culture. The Hieroglyphic Stairs, which is Copán's most famous site, has 62 steps and is covered with thousands of hieroglyphs that tell of Mayan history. The Acropolis contains several temples with altars carved with the images of ancient Mayan royalty. The Ball Court of Copán, where a Mayan ball game called "ollamalitzli" was played, is considered to be the second-largest Mayan Ball Court in existence. The Great Plaza holds many beautiful altars and statues. And finally, the Tunnels, which archaeologists dug under the Acropolis, shows evidence of earlier Mayan society buried underground.

Although Copán has been damaged by river erosion, earthquakes, and other natural events, it is still one of the most amazing sites of early American culture today.

Old Havana and Its Fortifications, Cuba
Cultural World Heritage Site since 1982

Photos of Havana, Cuba, show a city that appears to be lost in time. American cars from the 1950s roll down streets lined with colorful colonial buildings. On the bay stand forts and military buildings from the 16th century, and beyond the large port is the timeless sea. With its rich culture and its stormy history, Havana is perhaps one of the most interesting cities in the Americas.

Founded in 1519 by the Spanish, Havana was one of the last of the Cuban cities built by the Spanish. However, it soon became an important city in the Caribbean Sea and by 1607, it had become the capital of Cuba.

Several decades after being founded, Havana became the largest port in the Caribbean, and by the 17th century, it had become a major center for ship building. This was because Havana was the perfect stopping place for the ships carrying back to Spain all the gold and riches of Mexico, Peru, and the rest of the Americas. In this way, Cuba became the gateway to the vast Spanish empire, which made many an explorer and merchant very rich.

To protect the growing city, military buildings were built all around Havana between the 16th and 19th centuries. These buildings include some of the largest and oldest stone fortifications that exist in the Americas today.

Throughout the centuries, Cuba enjoyed much international trade. But in 1959, Fidel Castro and his army marched into Havana and took over the nation. Cuba became Communist, and it is now closed to much business with other countries.

Old Havana has five large plazas, and much of the city surrounding these plazas has stayed the same from the 19th and 20th centuries into present day. Impressive public buildings and historical treasures, such as the Iglesia Catedral de Le Habana and Palacio del Segundo Cabo, are located near the plazas. The Plaza de la Catedral is considered one of the most beautiful squares in the city. Today, Havana is home to a population of about two million people.

SOUTH AMERICA

Port, Fortresses, and Group of Monuments, Cartagena, Colombia p.76

Galápagos Islands, Ecuador p.68

Rapa Nui National Park, Chile p.78

Historic Sanctuary of Machu Picchu, Peru p.70

Iguazu National Park, Argentina and Brazil p.72

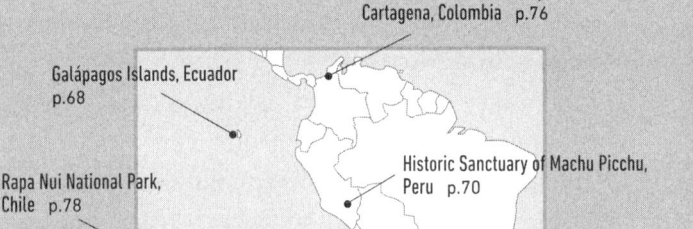

Los Glaciares National Park, Argentina p.74

Galápagos Islands, Ecuador
Natural World Heritage Site since 1978

Charles Darwin made these islands world famous when he studied the many plant and animal species here and came up with the theory of natural selection and evolution. Commonly called a "showcase of evolution," the Galápagos Islands hold some very special natural wonders.

Galápagos consists of 19 islands located about 1,000 kilometers west of Ecuador. This means the plant and animal species that live on the Galápagos Islands traveled 1,000 kilometers from nearby continental lands. And because the islands are so isolated, they evolved differently than their relatives back in South or Central America.

Three different ocean currents meet at the islands, mixing many species of sea animals at this particular spot. The islands were formed by volcanoes, which are still active today. All of these natural features gave rise to some very unique species that can only be seen on Galápagos. These include the Galápagos giant tortoise and its subspecies, the Galápagos penguin, the sea iguana, 13 species of Darwin's finches, and huge cacti, among many others.

Pinta Island, one of the Galápagos islands, was home to Lonesome George, a Pinta tortoise that was thought to be the last one left in the world. Sadly, Lonesome George died in June 2012, causing the world to believe that the species was gone from the earth forever. However, on one of the other Galápagos islands, scientists found 17 baby tortoises that appeared to be a mix of Pinta tortoise and a different tortoise. This led the scientists to believe that the babies' parents might still be alive, and therefore, the Pinta tortoise may not be extinct after all. Time and more study will answer this question.

Today, the number of visitors to the islands, over-fishing, and the introduction of invasive species are threatening the delicate balance of life on the Galápagos Islands. Because of this, the islands are under careful management to protect the islands' natural purity.

Historic Sanctuary of Machu Picchu, Peru

Cultural and Natural World Heritage Site since 1983

High up in the Andes Mountains of Peru sits one of the most amazing creations left behind by the Inca people. Machu Picchu, or "old peak" in the Quechua language, is a city located 2,430 meters above sea level. It sits on the top of a mountain in the middle of a tropical forest. Machu Picchu has become world-famous for its incredible setting, natural beauty, and impressive design.

The Inca Empire was the largest empire in the Americas before the arrival of Europeans. The capital was located where Cuzco sits in Peru today, but the empire stretched to Ecuador, Bolivia, Argentina, Chile, and even a small part of Colombia. The Incas were highly religious and believed the highest mountains of the Andes to be holy places.

Machu Picchu was built around 1450 but was abandoned about 100 years later, after Spanish colonists arrived in Peru. Although it is believed that the Spanish never found Machu Picchu, many of the Inca people who lived there may have died from foreign diseases brought by the Spanish. The world did not come to know about the Incan city until 1911, when the American historian named Hiram Bingham came across the site and was amazed by what he saw. Bingham traveled often to Peru because he was studying ancient cities in the area. On one of his trips, he was led to the site by an 11-year-old Peruvian boy. While the locals had known about Machu Picchu all along, Bingham made sure the rest of the world knew about it as well.

Although nobody knows for sure why Machu Picchu was built, it is believed to have been both a personal home for the Inca emperor Pachacuti as well as a holy site. There are many altars and temples in and around Machu Picchu that are evidence of religious activity. One theory for the location of Machu Picchu is that in addition to its striking natural beauty, the site lined up with key positions and events of the sun.

The city of Machu Picchu is divided into two

main areas, the city and its surrounding farms. The city was divided further into several districts: the district where the wise and holy men lived, the district where the king and his court lived, and the district where the farmers and common people lived. The three main sites at Machu Picchu are the Intihuatana stone (which is made to point directly at the sun during the winter and summer solstices), the Temple of the Sun, and the Room of Three Windows. More than 30 percent of Machu Picchu has been restored, and work on the ancient site continues today.

Iguazu National Park, Argentina and Brazil
Natural World Heritage Site since 1984

Iguazu Falls are considered by some to be the most beautiful waterfalls in the world. The falls measure 3 kilometers across and drop for about 80 meters in a series of steps. Shaped like a huge letter "J," the waterfalls are divided by many little islands. Creating a natural border between Argentina and Brazil, Iguazu Falls are shared by both countries.

Each country has its own national park surrounding the falls.

The word "Iguazu" (or "Iguaçu" on the Brazilian side) means "great water" in the local native language, and it is also the name of the river that feeds the falls. The Iguazu River is 1,320 kilometers long, winding mostly through Brazil. However, when the river drops suddenly off of a huge cliff, the waterfalls that form are mostly on the Argentinian side of the border.

The local people explain the waterfall with an old legend. According to the story, a god wanted to marry a beautiful young woman. But this woman fell in love with a young man and the couple decided to run away together. They got a boat and started to float down the river, but before long, the god found out. In great anger, the god cut the river in half, creating the waterfall and sending the young lovers falling to their death.

The fine mist created by the waterfalls creates a wet forest, in which many plants and animals thrive. The area is a particularly favorite spot for tropical birds. According to UNESCO, about half of Argentina's bird species can be found around Iguazu Falls. Today, the national parks on both sides of the waterfalls protect the plant and animals species in the area. However, careful management is needed to make sure the natural beauty and purity of the area is not threatened by nearby development and tourism.

Los Glaciares National Park, Argentina
Natural World Heritage Site since 1981

Los Glaciares National Park is Argentina's second-largest national park, but there is another reason why it is so special: it holds the world's largest ice cap outside of Antarctica and Greenland. The ice cap measures 14,000 square kilometers and feeds 47 active glaciers. There are also about 200 smaller glaciers that are not connected to the main ice sheet. About 30 percent of the park is covered in ice, and it is considered the best place in South America to witness active glaciers.

Los Glaciares is also home to many glacial lakes, including Lago Argentino (Argentinian Lake), the biggest freshwater lake in Argentina. Three active glaciers meet at Lago Argentino, creating frequent shows of huge icebergs crashing into the lake.

The cattle industry, which is a major economic force in South America, has turned much South American wilderness into grazing lands. This has led to many wild animal and bird populations decreasing or even becoming endangered. However, some of these animals find safety in Los Glaciares. The park's lakes make a perfect home for many birds. There are over 1,000 species of birds that live in the area, including swans, ducks, geese, and Chilean flamingoes. The park is also home to the endangered gray fox.

With its towering mountains, vast sheets of white ice, turquoise blue waters, and flocks of various birds, Los Glaciares is a special sight to see.

Port, Fortresses, and Group of Monuments, Cartagena, Colombia
Cultural World Heritage Site since 1984

Considered by some to be the most beautiful city in South America, Cartagena, the capital city of Colombia, is a historical treasure. Cartagena sits on Colombia's Caribbean coast, and because it was such an important port city in past centuries, it has the most military buildings in all of South America. It is also home to some of the best-preserved colonial architecture on the continent.

Cartagena was founded in 1533 by a Spanish explorer, Pedro de Heredia. The city was named after Cartagena, Spain, where many of Heredia's sailors were from. About 50 years later, Bautista Antonelli, the best military engineer in Spain, was hired to build fortifications at Cartagena. He worked for over a decade, turning Cartagena into a fort city that could last through any attack. Little by little, more forts and defenses were added to the city. Protected and sheltered against all dangers, the city continued to grow, becoming one of the richest and most important in the Caribbean. The city came to be known throughout South America as the continent's greatest example of Spanish military engineering.

Today, the city still holds much of its beauty from the colonial period. The narrow streets, wide plazas, brightly painted buildings, and historical monuments take one back to a different time.

Rapa Nui National Park, Chile
Cultural World Heritage Site since 1995

Rapa Nui is the Polynesian name of both Easter Island and the native people who occupied it. The Rapa Nui people are famous today as the creators of the Moai stone statues. They still live on the island today.

Easter Island is one of the most remote islands in the world. The closest continental land to Easter Island is Chile, but it is still 3,700 kilometers away. The Rapa Nui are believed to have begun living on the island in the first millennium AD. They came from Eastern Polynesia and quickly populated the island, creating a rich culture with impressive works of art and architecture.

The *moai* are believed to have been created between AD 1250 and 1500. They are huge human figures with large heads carved out of stone. Many *moai* were set upon huge stone altars called *ahu*. These *ahu* were arranged all along the edge of the island, and the *moai* look in toward land and the villages of the Rapa Nui. The *moai* are thought to represent the ancestors of the Rapa Nui, and they are arranged in this way perhaps to watch over and protect the people and their island.

Moai share similar traits, such as the large head, deep-set eyes, and broad nose. The tallest *moai* stands about 10 meters tall and weighs about 74,000 kilograms. The heaviest one is shorter, but weighs over 78,000 kilograms. There are 887 *moai* statues on Easter Island, although some are broken and some were never finished.

Some studies show that the Rapa Nui's culture began to decline around the 16th century due to decreasing natural resources. Europeans made contact with the Rapa Nui in the 18th century. Today, the Rapa Nui continue to live on Easter Island, but their culture has changed a lot after the effects of European contact. The population of the island now is about 2,000 people, counting both Chileans and the Rapa Nui.

Word List

- 本文で使われている全ての語を掲載しています (LEVEL 1、2)。ただし、LEVEL 3以上は、中学校レベルの語を含みません。
- 語形が規則変化する語の見出しは原形で示しています。不規則変化語は本文中で使われている形になっています。
- 一般的な意味を紹介していますので、一部の語で本文で実際に使われている品詞や意味と合っていないことがあります。
- 品詞は以下のように示しています。

名 名詞	代 代名詞	形 形容詞	副 副詞	動 動詞	助動 助動詞
前 前置詞	接 接続詞	間 間投詞	冠 冠詞	略 略語	俗 俗語
頭 接頭語	尾 接尾語	記 記号	関代 関係代名詞		

A

- **A.D.** 略 紀元後, 西暦~年 (= anno Domini)《ラテン語》
- **abandon** 動 放棄する
- **abbey** 名 修道院 Abbey of Saint Peter 聖ペーター僧院教会 Franciscan Abbey フランチェスコ会修道院聖堂
- **aboriginal** 名 先住民,《the A-》アボリジニ 形 先住民の,《the A-》アボリジニの
- **access** 名 接近, 近づく方法, 通路
- **accident** 熟 by accident 偶然に
- **accidentally** 副 偶然に
- **acropolis** 名 ①《the A-》(アテネの)アクロポリス《地名》②城砦
- **across** 熟 come across ~に出くわす, ~に遭遇する walk across ~を歩いて渡る
- **activity** 名 活動
- **actually** 副 実際に
- **addition** 熟 in addition 加えて, さらに
- **Adriatic Sea** アドリア海
- **advanced** 形 高等の
- **Africa** 名 アフリカ《大陸》
- **African** 形 アフリカ(人)の 名 アフリカ人
- **after all** やはり, 結局
- **after that** その後
- **ago** 熟 long ago ずっと前に, 昔
- **Agra** 名 アグラ《地名》
- **ahu** 名 アフー《石の祭壇》
- **Al Khazneh** エル・カズネ《宝物殿の意味, アラビア語》
- **all** 熟 after all やはり, 結局 all of which ~の中で all over ~中で, 全体にわたって
- **along witn** ~と一緒に
- **alpine** 形 高原の, アルプスの
- **Alps** 名 アルプス《地名》
- **altar** 名 祭壇
- **amaze** 動 びっくりさせる, 驚嘆させる
- **amazing** 形 驚くべき, 見事な
- **America** 名 アメリカ《国名・大陸》
- **American** 形 アメリカ(人)の 名 アメリカ人
- **Anatolian** 名 アナトリア人
- **ancestor** 名 祖先, 先祖
- **ancient** 形 昔の, 古代の

Word List

- **and so** それだから,それで
- **Andes** 图アンデス《地名》
- **Angkor** 图アンコール遺跡,アンコール王朝《かつて東南アジアに存在したクメール人の王国,9世紀-15世紀》
- **Angkor Archaeological Park** アンコール遺跡公園
- **Angkor Wat** アンコール・ワット《寺社遺跡》
- **Antarctica** 图南極
- **antelope** 图カモシカ
- **antler** 图(雄ジカの)枝角
- **any less** それでもやはり,~にもかかわらず
- **any time** いつでも
- **anyone** 代《否定文で》誰も(~ない)
- **Aotearoa** 图アオテアロア《白く長い雲のたなびく地の意味,マオリ語》
- **Apollo** 图アポロン《ギリシャ神話の男神》
- **appear to** ~するように見える
- **appreciate** 動正しく評価する,よさがわかる,ありがたく思う
- **appreciation** 图正しい評価,真価を認めること
- **Arab** 图アラビア人,アラブ民族,アラブ 形アラブ(人)の
- **Arabian** 形アラビアの
- **Aramean** 图アラム人,古代シリア人
- **archaeological** 形考古学の
- **archaeologist** 图考古学者
- **architect** 图建築家,設計者
- **architectural** 形建築上の
- **architecture** 图建築(学),建築物(様式)
- **Argentina** 图アルゼンチン《国名》
- **Argentinian** 形アルゼンチンの
- **Arizona** 图アリゾナ州
- **Armenian** 形アルメニア人の
- **arrange** 動並べる,配置する
- **arrival** 图到達
- **arrive in** ~に着く
- **art** 熟 works of art 芸術作品
- **artist** 图芸術家
- **artistic** 形芸術的な,芸術(家)の
- **artwork** 图芸術作品
- **as** 熟 as best one can 精一杯,できるだけ as soon as ~するとすぐ,~するや否や as to ~に関しては,~については as well なお,その上,同様に as well as ~と同様に,~に加えて such as たとえば~,~のような
- **Ashoka** 图アショーカ《古代インドの王,前268頃-前232頃》
- **Asia** 图アジア
- **aside** 熟 aside from ~だけでなく put aside ~を無視する,わきに置く
- **Askia the Great** アスキア大王《ソンガイ帝国の王,1443頃-1529頃》
- **Assyrian** 图アッシリア人
- **astronomy** 图天文学
- **Athena** 图アテナ《ギリシャ神話の女神》
- **Athens** 图アテネ《地名》
- **Atlantic** 形大西洋の 图《the-》大西洋
- **attach** 動付着する
- **attract** 動引きつける,魅了する
- **Auschwitz** 图アウシュビッツ《地名》,アウシュビッツ強制収容所
- **Australia** 图オーストラリア《国名》
- **Australian** 形オーストラリアの
- **Austria** 图オーストリア《国名》
- **Avalokitasvara** 観音菩薩
- **Avebury** 图エイヴバリー《地名》

WORLD HERITAGE SITE TOP 38

- **Avenue** 名アベニュー《古代道路の遺跡》

B

- **B.C.** 略紀元前, 紀元前〜年（=Before Christ）
- **back** 熟 back and forth あちこちへ　take 〜 back to ①〜を…へ持ち帰る ②〜を…に引き戻す
- **Banff** 名バンフ《地名》
- **Baroque period** バロック時代《16世紀末–17世紀初頭》
- **based on** 《be–》〜に基づく
- **battery** 名砲台 Six-Gun Battery 六連砲台
- **Bautista Antonelli** バウティスタ・アントネッリ《要塞建築家, 1547–1616》
- **Bayon** 名バイヨン《アンコール遺跡にある寺院跡》
- **Beaker** 名ビーカー人《銅器や大型杯（ビーカー）を扱っていた人々》
- **because of** 〜のために, 〜の理由で
- **bed** 名地層
- **before long** やがて, まもなく
- **belief** 名信念
- **Belize** 名ベリーズ《国名》
- **Benedictine Abbey** ベネディクト修道院
- **best** 熟 as best one can 精一杯, できるだけ
- **best-preserved** 形保存状態の極めて良い
- **Bible** 名《the –》聖書
- **billion** 形10億の, ばく大な, 無数の 名10億
- **biologically** 副生物学的に
- **Birkenau** 名ビルケナウ《地名》, ビルケナウ絶滅収容所
- **birth** 名出産, 誕生 give birth to 〜を生む
- **birthplace** 名出生地
- **bishop** 名司教, 主教
- **blend** 名混合物
- **bodhisattva** 名菩薩
- **bold** 形力強い, 派手な
- **Bolivia** 名ボリビア《国名》
- **book-making** 名書籍製造
- **book-selling** 名書籍販売
- **both A and B** A も B も
- **Brazil** 名ブラジル《国》
- **Brazilian** 形ブラジル（人）の
- **brick** 名レンガ, レンガ状のもの
- **brightly** 副明るく
- **bring to mind** 〜を思い起こさせる
- **bring up** 指摘する, 提示する
- **British** 形英国人の
- **Buddha** 名仏陀, 釈迦《仏教の開祖》
- **Buddhist** 形仏教（徒）の 名仏教徒
- **Buktu** 名ブクトゥ《人名》
- **Burgess Shale** バージェス頁岩《古生代カンブリア紀の化石を閉じ込めた堆積層》
- **burial** 名埋葬
- **bury** 動①埋葬する, 埋める ②覆い隠す
- **by the time** 〜する時までに
- **by then** その時までに
- **Byzantine** 形ビザンチン帝国の 名ビザンチウムの住人

C

- **cacti** 名 cuctus（サボテン）の複数
- **calcite** 名方解石, カルサイト《石

灰岩・大理石の主成分》
- **call to mind** 思い浮かべる
- **calligraphy** 名書法, 筆跡
- **Cambodia** 名カンボジア《国名》
- **camel** 名ラクダ
- **can** 熟 **as best one can** 精一杯, できるだけ
- **Canada** 名カナダ《国名》
- **Canadian** 形カナダ(人)の
- **canal** 名用水路, 運河
- **canyon** 名峡谷, 深い谷
- **capture** 動①捕える ②(永続的な形で)保存する
- **Carcassonne** 名カルカソンヌ《地名》
- **care for** 〜の世話をする, 〜の手入れをする
- **Caribbean** 形カリブ海の, 西インド諸島の
- **carnival** 名謝肉祭, カーニバル
- **Cartagena** 名カルタヘナ《地名》
- **carve** 動彫る, 彫刻する
- **cathedral** 名大聖堂
- **cattle** 名畜牛, 家畜
- **cave** 名洞穴, 洞窟
- **cave system** 洞窟
- **Celsius** 名セ氏温度計, ℃
- **cemetery** 名共同墓地
- **Cenozoic** 名新生代《約6,500万年前–現代》
- **centimeter** 名センチメートル《長さの単位》
- **central** 形中央の
- **certainly** 副確実に
- **chamber** 名部屋, 室 **gas chamber** (殺傷用の)ガス室
- **chariot** 名(古代の)二輪馬車の戦車
- **Charles Darwin** チャールズ・ダーウィン《イギリスの博物学者, 1809–82》
- **charming** 形魅力的な, うっとりさせるような
- **cheetah** 名チーター
- **Chile** 名チリ《国名》
- **Chilean** 名チリ人 形チリの
- **China** 名中国《国名》
- **Chinese** 形中国(人)の
- **Christian** 名キリスト教徒, クリスチャン 形キリスト(教)の
- **Christianity** 名キリスト教, キリスト教信仰
- **Church of the Holy Sepulchre** 聖墳墓教会
- **circle** 熟 **stone circle** 環状列石, ストーンサークル
- **city-state** 名都市国家
- **civil** 形国内の, 国家の **civil war** 内戦, 内乱
- **civilization** 名文明, 文明人(化)
- **Claude Monet** クロード・モネ《フランスの画家, 1840–1926》
- **clay** 名粘土
- **clever** 形利口な
- **cliff** 名断崖, 絶壁
- **climate** 名気候, 風土
- **close by** すぐ近くに
- **clue** 名手がかり, 糸口
- **collection** 名集まり, 堆積
- **Colombia** 名コロンビア《国名》
- **colonial** 形植民地の
- **colonist** 名入植者
- **colony** 名①植民[移民](地) ②コロニー《同じ種類の動植物が共生する集団》
- **Colorado River** コロラド川
- **colorful** 形カラフルな, 生き生きとした
- **combination** 名結合体
- **combine** 動結びつく, 結合する

WORLD HERITAGE SITE TOP 38

- **come** 熟 come across ～に出くわす, ～に遭遇する come into contact with ～と接触する come up 生じる come up with ～を思いつく, 考え出す
- **commonly** 副 一般に, 通例
- **communist** 名 共産主義者
- **compare** 動 比較する, 対照する
- **completely** 副 完全に
- **concentration camp** 強制収容所
- **conflict** 名 衝突, 争い
- **connect** 動 つながる, 結びつける, 結合する
- **conservation** 名 保護, 保存 World Conservation Union 国際自然保護連合
- **conservationist** 名 自然保護活動家
- **consist** 動 《– of ～》(部分・要素から) 成る
- **constant** 形 絶えない, 持続する
- **construction** 名 建設, 工事
- **contact** 熟 come into contact with ～と接触する
- **continent** 名 大陸, 陸地
- **continental** 形 大陸の Continental divide ロッキー山脈分水界
- **continually** 副 継続的に, 絶えず
- **Copán** 名 コパン《マヤ文明の大都市》
- **coral** 名 サンゴ (珊瑚) 形 サンゴの coral reef サンゴ礁
- **cotton** 名 綿, 綿花
- **council** 名 会議 International Council on Monuments and Sites 国際記念物世界会議
- **countless** 形 無数の, 数え切れない
- **county** 名 郡, 州
- **courtyard** 名 中庭
- **covered with** 《be –》～でおおわれている
- **craft** 名 手工業, 工芸
- **creation** 名 創造 (物)
- **creative** 形 創造力のある, 独創的な
- **creator** 名 創作者, 考案者
- **criteria** 名 基準
- **cross-piece** 名 桟, 横木
- **crossroad** 名 交差道路, 十字路
- **crown** 名 王冠
- **cruelty** 名 残酷な行為
- **crusade** 名 《C-》十字軍, 聖戦 Indiana Jones and the Last Crusade 『インディ・ジョーンズ/最後の聖戦』(アメリカ映画, 1989)
- **Cuba** 名 キューバ《国名》
- **Cuban** 形 キューバの
- **cultural** 形 文化の, 文化的な Cultural and Natural World Heritage Site 世界文化自然遺産 Cultural World Heritage Site 世界文化遺産
- **culturally** 副 文化的に
- **cure** 動 治療する, 取り除く
- **currently** 副 現在
- **Cursus** 名 カーサス《巨大な溝の遺跡》
- **cut through** 切り開く
- **Cuzco** 名 クスコ《インカ帝国の古代都市》
- **cycle** 名 周期, 循環

D

- **Dahshur** 名 ダハシュール遺跡《王家の墓地》
- **Damascus** 名 ダマスカス《シリアの首都》
- **David Livingstone** デイヴィ

Word List

ッド・リビングストン《スコットランドの探検家, 1813-1873》
- **Dead Sea** 死海
- **decade** 名 10年間
- **decision** 名 決定
- **decorate** 動 装飾する
- **decrease** 動 減少する
- **dedicate** 動 捧げる, 奉納する
- **deed** 名 行為
- **deeply** 副 深く, 非常に
- **deep-set** 形 落ち窪んだ
- **deer** 名 シカ(鹿)
- **delicate** 形 繊細な, 壊れやすい
- **desert** 名 砂漠
- **desertification** 名 砂漠化
- **desert-like** 形 砂漠状態の
- **desirable** 形 好ましい, 魅力がある
- **despite** 前 ～にもかかわらず
- **destination** 名 行き先, 目的地
- **Devadaha** 名 デーヴァダハ《地名》
- **development** 名 開発, 発展
- **devote** 動 (～を…に)捧げる
- **differently** 副 (～と)異なって
- **dig** 動 掘る, 掘り返す **dig up** 掘り起こす, 掘り出す
- **direction** 名 方向, 方角
- **directly** 副 まさに, ちょうどに
- **diverse** 形 種々の, 多様な
- **divide into** ～に分かれる
- **Djoser** 名 ジョセル《古代エジプトの王, 紀元前2600年頃》
- **dolphin** 名 イルカ
- **Dome of the Rock** 名 岩のドーム《イスラム教のモスク》
- **drop off** ～から(取れて)落ちる
- **due to** ～によって, ～が原因で
- **dug** 動 dig(掘る)の過去, 過去分詞
- **Durrington Walls** ダーリントン・ウォールズ《集落遺跡》
- **dynasty** 名 王朝[王家](の統治期間)

E

- **earth** 熟 **on earth** 地球上で, この世で
- **earthquake** 名 地震
- **Easter Island** イースター島
- **eastern** 形 東の, 東洋の
- **ecosystem** 名 生態系
- **Ecuador** 名 エクアドル《国名》
- **Edgar Degas** エドガー・ドガ《フランスの画家, 1834-1917》
- **Egypt** 名 エジプト《国名》
- **Egyptian** 形 エジプト(人)の 名 エジプト人
- **either A or B** AかそれともB
- **El Salvador** エルサルバドル《国名》
- **emperor** 名 皇帝, 天皇
- **empire** 名 帝国
- **employ** 動 (人を)雇う, 使う
- **empress** 名 女帝, 女性天皇
- **enchanting** 形 魅力的な
- **end** 熟 **at the end of** ～の終わりに
- **endangered** 形 絶滅寸前の
- **engineer** 名 技師
- **engineering** 名 工学
- **England** 名 ①イングランド ②英国
- **enlightenment** 名 悟り
- **enormous** 形 巨大な
- **enough to do** ～するのに十分な
- **entertainer** 名 楽しませる人
- **environment** 名 環境

WORLD HERITAGE SITE TOP 38

- **environmental** 形環境の
- **era** 名時代, 年代
- **Erechtheion** 名エレクテイオン《神殿》
- **erosion** 名浸食
- **estimate** 動見積もる
- **Eugene-Emmanuel Viollet-le-Duc** ウジェーヌ・エマニュエル・ヴィオレ・ル・デュク《フランスの建築家, 1814-1879》
- **Europe** 名ヨーロッパ
- **European** 名ヨーロッパ人 形ヨーロッパ(人)の
- **ever since** それ以来ずっと
- **everywhere** 副いずれの場所においても
- **evolution** 名進化
- **evolve** 動進化する
- **existence** 名現存
- **explorer** 名探検者[家]
- **extermination camp** 絶滅収容所
- **extinct** 形絶滅した
- **extreme** 形行き過ぎた, 極度の

F

- **fact** 熟 in fact つまり, 要するに, 実は
- **fairy tale** おとぎ話
- **fall** 動落ちる, 倒れる, 滅びる fall in love with 恋におちる 名《-s》滝
- **far-away** 形遥か彼方の
- **farmer** 名農民
- **fascinating** 形魅惑的な, うっとりさせるような
- **fed** 動 feed (供給する)の過去, 過去分詞
- **Fidel Castro** フィデル・カストロ《キューバの革命家, 1926-》
- **figure out** 理解する, (原因などを)解明する
- **filled with** 《be -》~でいっぱいになる
- **finch** 名フィンチ《アトリ科スズメ目の鳥の総称》
- **find out** 見つける, 気がつく
- **finding** 名《-s》発見物, 調査結果
- **flamingo** 名フラミンゴ
- **float** 動①浮く, 浮かぶ ②漂流する
- **flock** 名(鳥などの)群れ
- **flood** 名洪水
- **focus** 名中心
- **foot** 熟 at the foot of ~のすそ[下部]に
- **for a while** しばらくの間, 少しの間
- **for sure** 確かに
- **formation** 名形成
- **fort** 名砦, 要塞 Fort Bullen バレン要塞
- **forth** 熟 back and forth あちこちへ
- **fortification** 名要塞
- **fortify** 動要塞化する
- **fortress** 名要塞
- **fossil** 名化石
- **fox** 名キツネ(狐) gray fox ハイイロギツネ
- **France** 名フランス《国名》
- **Franciscan Abbey** フランチェスコ会修道院聖堂
- **Frank** 名フランク人《ゲルマン人の一支族》
- **French** 形フランス(人)の
- **freshwater** 形真水の, 淡水の
- **from this point on** この地点から先は
- **frozen** 形凍った
- **Fuji-san** 名富士山

Word List

- **Fujisan Hongu Sengen Taisha** 富士山本宮浅間大社
- **fulfill** 動 (義務・約束を)果たす
- **full of** 《be –》~で一杯である
- **fully** 副 十分に, 完全に

G

- **Galápagos Islands** ガラパゴス諸島
- **Gambia** 名 ガンビア《国名》
- **Gansu Province** 甘粛省《地名》
- **gas chamber** (殺傷用の)ガス室
- **gateway** 名 玄関口
- **gazelle** 名 ガゼル
- **geese** 名 goose (ガチョウ)の複数
- **geological** 形 地質学の
- **German** 形 ドイツ(人)の 名 ドイツ人
- **Germanic** 形 ゲルマン民族の
- **Germany** 名 ドイツ《国名》
- **get to** ~に達する[到着する]
- **giant** 形 巨大な
- **give birth to** ~を生む
- **give rise to** ~を引き起こす
- **Giza** 名 ギザ《地名》
- **glacial** 形 氷河の
- **glacier** 名 氷河
- **go into** (事業など)に参入する
- **go on** (時間が)たつ, 経過する
- **go through** しかるべき手順を踏む, 体験する
- **goddess** 名 女神
- **Golden Hall** 金堂《仏殿》
- **gondola** 名 ゴンドラ
- **goods** 名 商品, 品物
- **gorge** 名 峡谷, 山峡
- **Gothic** 形 ゴシック建築の
- **government** 名 政府
- **Grand Canyon National Park** グランド・キャニオン国立公園
- **grandness** 名 雄大さ
- **grass** 名 草地
- **grassland** 名 草原
- **gray fox** ハイイロギツネ
- **grazing** 名 牧草地
- **Great Barrier Reef** グレート・バリア・リーフ《世界最大のサンゴ礁地帯》
- **Great Britain** グレート・ブリテン(島)
- **Great Wall** 万里の長城
- **Greece** 名 ギリシア《国名》
- **Greek** 形 ギリシア(人)の 名 ①ギリシア人 ②ギリシア語
- **Greenland** 名 グリーンランド《地名》
- **Guatemala** 名 グアテマラ《国名》

H

- **Hamber** 名 ハンバー《地名》
- **harm** 名 損害
- **hate** 名 憎しみ
- **Havana** 名 ハバナ《キューバの首都》
- **Hawaii** 名 ハワイ《米国の州》
- **heal** 動 いやす, 治す
- **healthy** 形 健やかな
- **hear of** ~について聞く
- **heartbroken** 形 悲しみに打ちひしがれた
- **heavily** 副 厳しく
- **herd** 名 (大型動物の)一群
- **heritage** 名 遺産 World Heritage 世界遺産 World Heritage Committee 世界遺産委員会

WORLD HERITAGE SITE TOP 38

- **Herod Agrippa** ヘロデ・アグリッパ1世《古代ユダヤの統治者, 紀元前10–44》
- **Hierapolis** 名 ヒエラポリス《古代ローマ帝国の都市》
- **Hierapolis-Pamukkale** 名 ヒエラポリス-パムッカレ《石灰石の丘陵地》
- **hieroglyph** 名 象形文字
- **hieroglyphic** 形 象形文字の
- **highly** 副 非常に
- **high-quality** 形 高品質の
- **Himalaya Mountain** ヒマラヤ山脈
- **Hindu** 名 ヒンドゥー人, ヒンドゥー教信者
- **Hiram Bingham** ハイラム・ビンガム《アメリカの探検家, 政治家, 1875–1956》
- **hire** 動 雇う
- **historian** 名 歴史家
- **historic** 形 歴史上有名[重要]な, 歴史的な
- **historical** 形 歴史の, 歴史上の
- **holocaust** 名 大虐殺, ホロコースト
- **holy** 形 聖なる, 神聖な
- **Honduras** 名 ホンジュラス《国名》
- **honor** 熟 in honor of ~を記念して, ~に敬意を表して
- **Horyu-ji** 名 法隆寺
- **humanity** 名 人間性, 人間らしさ
- **humble** 形 つつましい, 粗末な
- **Hundred Years' War** 百年戦争《1337–1453》
- **hundreds of** 何百もの~
- **hunting-and-gathering** 形 狩猟と採集の
- **Hushan Great Wall** 虎山長城《中国明代の遺構》
- **Huta-Ka-Ptah** 名 フゥト・カー・プタハ《プタハ神の魂の神殿》

I

- **iceberg** 名 氷山
- **Iglesia Catedral de Le Habana** ハバナ大聖堂
- **Iguazu National Park** イグアス国立公園
- **Ikaruga** 名 斑鳩《地名》
- **illness** 名 病気
- **image** 名 印象, 姿
- **imagination** 名 想像(力), 空想
- **immediately** 副 すぐに
- **importance** 名 重要性, 大切さ
- **impressionist** 形 印象派の
- **impressive** 形 印象的な, 感動的な
- **Inca** 名 インカ《南アメリカに存在した王国, 1438–1527》
- **Incan** 名 インカ人
- **including** 前 ~を含めて, 込みで
- **incredible** 形 信じられない, すばらしい, とてつもない
- **incredibly** 副 信じられないほど, 途方もなく
- **India** 名 インド《国名》
- **Indian** 形 インド(人)の
- **Indiana Jones and the Last Crusade** 『インディ・ジョーンズ/最後の聖戦』(アメリカ映画, 1989)
- **influential** 形 影響力の大きい, 有力な
- **inhabit** 動 ①(ある場所に)住む, 居住する ②~に存在する
- **insect** 名 虫, 昆虫
- **inspiration** 名 ひらめき
- **instead of** ~の代わりに, ~をしないで

Word List

- **institutionalize** 動 慣行化する,制度化する
- **International Council on Monuments and Sites** 国際記念物世界会議
- **Intihuatana** 名 インティワタナ《太陽をつなぎとめる石の意味,ケチュア語》
- **invader** 名 侵略国,侵略軍
- **invasive** 形 侵略的な
- **Islam** 名 イスラム教[教徒・文化]
- **Islamic** 形 イスラムの,イスラム教の
- **isolated** 形 隔離した,孤立した
- **Italian** 形 イタリア(人)の 名 イタリア人
- **Italy** 名 イタリア《国名》
- **ivory** 名 象牙

J

- **James Island** ジェームズ島
- **Japan** 名 日本《国名》
- **Japanese** 形 日本(人)の
- **Jasper** 名 ジャスパー《地名》
- **Jayavarman VII** ジャヤーヴァルマン7世《クメール王朝の王,1125-1218頃》
- **jellyfish** 名 クラゲ
- **Jerusalem** 名 エルサレム《地名》
- **Jew** 名 ユダヤ人,ユダヤ教徒
- **jewel** 名 宝石
- **Jewish** 形 ユダヤ人の,ユダヤ教の
- **Jiayuguan City** 嘉峪関《地名》
- **Jordan** 名 ヨルダン《国名》
- **Judaism** 名 ユダヤ教
- **Judean Mountains** ジュデアン・マウンテンズ《地名》

K

- **Kakadu National Park** カカドゥ国立公園
- **Katsushika Hokusai** 葛飾北斎《江戸時代後期の浮世絵師,1760-1849》
- **Khafra** 名 カフラー《古代エジプトの王,?-紀元前2480》
- **Khmer** 名 クメール人《カンボジアを中心とする東南アジアの民族》
- **kilogram** 名 キログラム《重量の単位》
- **kilometer** 名 キロメートル《長さの単位》
- **kingdom** 名 王国
- **Kiribati** 名 キリバス《国名》
- **known as** 《be -》~として知られている
- **Kololo** 名 コロロ族《アフリカ南部に住むバントゥー系民族の一つ》
- **Kootenay** 名 クートニー《地名》
- **Kunta Kinteh Island** クンタ・キンテ島

L

- **Lago Argentino** アルヘンチノ湖
- **lagoon** 名 潟
- **Laguna Veneta** ヴェネタ潟《地名》
- **Lake Kawaguchi** 河口湖
- **Lake Yamanaka** 山中湖
- **landmark** 名 ランドマーク,歴史的建造物
- **landscape** 名 景色,風景
- **lava** 名 溶岩
- **lead to** ~を引き起こす
- **least** 熟 at least 少なくとも

World Heritage Site Top 38

- leave behind ～を置き去りにする
- leave in ～をそのままにしておく
- led 動 lead(導く)の過去, 過去分詞
- legend 名 伝説, 言い伝え
- legendary 形 有名な
- less 熟 any less それでもやはり, ～にもかかわらず
- Liaoning Province 遼寧省
- life-sized 形 等身大の
- lifestyle 名 生活様式, ライフスタイル
- like 熟 look like ～のように見える, ～に似ている
- limestone 名 石灰岩
- line up with ～とぴったりと合う
- lined with 《be –》～が立ち並ぶ
- list 熟 put ～ on a list ～をリストに載せる
- liter 名 リットル, リッター《容積の単位》
- literature 名 文学, 文芸
- little by little 少しずつ
- live on 生き続ける, ～に住む
- living quarter 居住区
- living thing 生物
- locate 動 置く, 位置づける, 本拠地とする
- location 名 位置, 場所
- lonesome 形 さびしい
- Lonesome George ロンサム・ジョージ《ピンタゾウガメ最後の生き残りの愛称》
- long 熟 before long やがて, まもなく long ago ずっと前に, 昔
- look 熟 look down on ～を見下ろす look for ～を探す look like ～のように見える, ～に似ている look over ～を見渡す
- Los Glaciares National Park ロス・グラシアレス国立公園
- love 熟 fall in love with 恋におちる
- lover 名 恋人
- Lumbini 名 ルンビニ《地名》

M

- Maasai 名 マサイ族《ケニア, タンザニアの先住民族》
- Machu Picchu マチュ・ピチュ《インカ帝国の遺跡》
- make 熟 be made of ～でできて[作られて]いる be made to ～させられる make out 作り上げる make sure 確かめる, 確認する, 確実に～になるようにする make up 作り出す, ～を構成[形成]する make ～ into ～を…に仕立てる
- Mali 名 マリ《国名》
- mammal 名 哺乳動物
- management 名 管理, 取り扱い
- man-made 形 人工の
- Maori 名 マオリ族《ニュージーランドのポリネシア系先住民》
- marble 名 大理石
- marketplace 名 市場, 市がたつ広場
- matter 熟 no matter ～を問わず plant matter 植物
- Maurel Frères Building モーレル兄弟の商館
- mausoleum 名 霊廟
- Maya 名 マヤ人《アメリカ先住民族》
- Maya Devi 摩耶夫人《仏陀の母》
- Mayan 形 マヤの, マヤ人の
- meadow 名 牧草地, 草地
- meaning 名 意味, 重要性

Word List

- **medieval** 形 中世の
- **Mediterranean** 形 地中海（沿岸）の 名《the M-》地中海
- **melting pot** るつぼ
- **Memphis** 名 メンフィス《地名》
- **Menes** 名 メネス《初代ファラオといわれている人物, 紀元前3000年頃》
- **merchant** 名 商人, 貿易商
- **Mesozoic** 名 中生代《約2億5千百万年前−6,550万年前》
- **meter** 名 メートル《長さの単位》
- **Mexico** 名 メキシコ《国名》
- **mid** 頭 中頃の
- **middle** 熟 in the middle of ～の真ん中[中ほど]に
- **migration** 名 移動
- **military** 形 軍隊[軍人]の, 軍事の
- **millennium** 名 千年間
- **minaret** 名（イスラム寺院の）尖塔
- **mind** 熟 bring to mind ～を思い起こさせる call to mind 思い浮かべる
- **mineral** 名 鉱物, 鉱石
- **Ming Dynasty** 明王朝《中国の王朝の一つ, 1368–1644》
- **mist** 名 霧, かすみ
- **moai** 名 モアイ《石像彫刻》
- **mollusk** 名 軟体動物
- **monastery** 名 修道院, 僧院
- **monk** 名 修道士, 僧
- **Mont Saint-Michel** モン・サン＝ミッシェル《地名, 修道院名》
- **monument** 名 記念碑, 遺跡
- **moonbow** 名 月光虹
- **more than** ～以上
- **Mosi-oa-Tunya** 名 モーシ・オワ・トゥーニャ《雷鳴の轟く水煙の意味, バントゥー語》
- **mosque** 名 モスク, イスラム教寺院
- **mostly** 副 大部分は, 主に
- **Mount Assiniboine** 名 マウント・アシニボイン
- **Mount Meru** メル山, 須弥山《古代インドの世界観の中心にある架空の山》
- **Mount Ngauruhoe** ナウルホエ山
- **Mount Robson** マウント・ロブソン
- **Mount Ruapehu** ルアペフ山
- **Mountain Li** 驪山
- **move on** 前進する
- **Mughal** 名 ムガル帝国《かつてインドに存在したイスラム国家, 1526–1858》
- **Muhammad** 名 ムハンマド《イスラム教の開祖, 570年頃−632》
- **Mumtaz Mahal** ムムターズ・マハル《ムガル帝国の皇妃, 1595–1631》
- **museum** 名 博物館
- **musician** 名 音楽家
- **Muslim** 名 イスラム教徒, ムスリム
- **mystery** 名 神秘, 不可思議

N

- **Nabatean** 名 ナバテア人《北アラビアを起源とする遊牧民族》
- **name after** ～にちなんで名付ける
- **Nara Prefecture** 奈良県
- **national** 形 国立の, 国家の, 国民的な
- **native** 形 ①出生（地）の, 土地の ②（～に）固有の, 生まれつきの
- **Nazi** ナチス, 国家社会党（員）
- **nearby** 形 近くの, 間近の 副 近くで

WORLD HERITAGE SITE TOP 38

- □ **necropolis** 名(古代の壮大な)共同墓地
- □ **Nepal** 名ネパール《国名》
- □ **nephew** 名おい(甥)
- □ **network** 名道路網, ネットワーク
- □ **New Zealand** 名ニュージーランド《国名》
- □ **news** 名ニュース, 知らせ
- □ **next to** 〜のとなりに
- □ **Nile River** ナイル川
- □ **no matter** 〜を問わず
- □ **nobody** 代誰も[1人も]〜ない
- □ **nomadic** 形遊牧民の
- □ **nominate** 動指名する, 推薦する
- □ **Non-Aryan** 形アーリア人でない
- □ **Nonnberg Benedictine Nunnery** ノンベルク修道院
- □ **Normandy** 名ノルマンディー《地名》
- □ **northeast** 名北東(部)
- □ **northern** 形北の, 北からの
- □ **northwest** 名北西(部)
- □ **number of** 《a-》いくつかの〜, 多くの〜
- □ **nunnery** 名女子修道院

O

- □ **Occident** 名西洋
- □ **Oceania** 名オセアニア《地名》
- □ **octagon-shaped** 形八角形の
- □ **officially** 副公式に, 正式に
- □ **ollamalitzli** 名アステカ文明のバスケットボールに似た球技
- □ **once-great** 形かつての偉大な
- □ **one-of-a-kind** 形ユニークな, 独特の
- □ **onto** 前〜の上へ[に]
- □ **organization** 名組織, 機関 United Nations Educational, Scientific and Cultural Organization 国際連合教育科学文化機関, ユネスコ
- □ **Orient** 名東洋
- □ **originally** 副は, 元来
- □ **Oshino Hakkai** 忍野八海《湧泉群》
- □ **Ottoman** 形オスマン帝国の
- □ **out of** 〜から作り出して, 〜を材料として
- □ **over** 熟 all over 〜中で, 全体にわたって over time 時間とともに, そのうち
- □ **over-fishing** 名乱獲
- □ **overhead** 形頭上に, 真上に
- □ **overseas** 形海外の, 外国の

P

- □ **Pachacuti** 名パチャクテク《かつてアンデス山脈に存在したクスコ王国の王, ?-1471》
- □ **Pacific** 名太平洋
- □ **painful** 形痛ましい
- □ **painting** 名絵(をかくこと), 絵画
- □ **palace** 名宮殿, 大邸宅
- □ **Palacio del Segundo Cabo** 副総裁の宮殿《スペイン語》
- □ **Palaeozoic** 名古生代《約5億4千2百万年前−2億5千百万年前》
- □ **Pammukale** 名パムッカレ《石灰岩の丘陵地》
- □ **parent** 名《-s》両親
- □ **Parthenon** 名パルテノン神殿
- □ **particularly** 副特に, とりわけ
- □ **pass through** 〜を通る, 通行する
- □ **path** 名①歩道 ②進路, 通路
- □ **Paul Gauguin** ポール・ゴーギャ

Word List

ン《フランスの画家, 1848–1903》
- **pavilion** 名 館, パビリオン
- **peak** 名 頂点, 最高点
- **Pedro de Heredia** ペドロ・デ・エレディア《スペインの建築家, 1505–1554》
- **penguin** 名 ペンギン
- **per** 前 ～につき, ～ごとに
- **Pericles** 名 ペリクレス《古代アテネの政治家, 前495頃–前429》
- **Peru** 名 ペルー《国名》
- **Peruvian** 形 ペルー人の
- **Petra** 名 ペトラ《地名, 遺跡》
- **pharaoh** 名 王, ファラオ《古代エジプト王の称号》
- **Phoenix Islands** フェニックス諸島
- **photo** 名 写真
- **Pierre-Auguste Renoir** ピエール=オーギュスト・ルノワール《フランスの画家, 1841–1919》
- **pilgrim** 名 巡礼者
- **Pinta Island** ピンタ島
- **planning** 名 立案, 開発計画
- **plant matter** 植物
- **plateau** 名 台地, 高原
- **Plaza de la Catedral** カテドラル広場
- **poet** 名 詩人, 歌人
- **point** 熟 from this point on この地点から先は
- **Poland** 名 ポーランド《国名》
- **political** 形 政治の, 国政の
- **Polynesia** 名 ポリネシア《地名》
- **Polynesian** 形 ポリネシア(人)の
- **pool** 名 水たまり
- **populate** 動 居住させる
- **port** 名 港, 港町
- **Portuguese** 形 ポルトガル(人)の 名 ポルトガル人
- **Poseidon** 名 ポセイドン《ギリシャ神話の神》
- **possibly** 副 おそらく
- **pottery** 名 陶器
- **prayer** 名 祈り, 祈願
- **Precambrian** 名 先カンブリア時代《46億年前–5億年前》
- **precious** 形 貴重な, 大事な
- **prefecture** 名 県, 府
- **prehistoric** 形 有史以前の
- **present-day** 形 現代の
- **preserve** 動 守る, 保存する
- **pride** 名 誇り, 自慢
- **prophet** 名 預言者
- **Propylaea** 名 プロピュライア《門の遺跡》
- **protection** 名 保護, 防護物
- **protective** 形 保護する, 保護(用)の
- **proven** 動 prove (証明する)の過去分詞
- **province** 名 州, 省
- **public** 形 公共の
- **purity** 名 汚れのないこと, 純粋
- **put ~ on a list** ～をリストに載せる
- **put aside** ～を無視する, わきに置く
- **pyramid** 名 ピラミッド

Q

- **Qin** 秦《中国の古代王朝, 紀元前221–202》
- **quarter** 名 地区, 地域
- **Quechua** 名 ケチュア族《かつてインカ帝国を興した民族》
- **quickly** 副 すぐに

R

- **rainbow** 名 虹
- **Ramses** 名 ラムセス1世《古代エジプトの王》
- **Ramses II** ラムセス2世《古代エジプトの王, 前1314頃–前1224頃》
- **rank** 名 階級, 位
- **Rapa Nui** ラパ・ヌイ《イースター島の現地語名》, ラパ・ヌイ族《イースター島に住む民族》
- **rare** 形 まれな, 珍しい
- **reach for** ～に手を伸ばす
- **reality** 熟 in reality 実際には
- **rebuilt** 動 rebuild (再建する) の過去, 過去分詞
- **recently** 副 近ごろ, 最近
- **recommendation** 名 推薦(状)
- **Red Sea** 紅海
- **reef** 名 暗礁, 岩礁 coral reef サンゴ礁
- **reflect** 動 反映する, 示す
- **relate** 動 ①関係がある ②仲良くする
- **relative** 名 親戚, 同族
- **relic** 名 遺跡, 遺物
- **religion** 名 宗教, ～教
- **religious** 形 ①宗教の ②信心深い
- **remain** 動 (～の)ままである[いる]
- **remind** 動 思い出させる, 気づかせる
- **remote** 形 (距離・時間的に)遠い, 遠隔の
- **rename** 動 新しい名前をつける, 改名する
- **repeatedly** 副 繰り返して, たびたび
- **representation** 名 絵画, 肖像, 描写
- **republic** 名 共和国
- **resident** 名 居住者, 在住者
- **resource** 名 資源
- **restoration** 名 回復, 修復
- **restore** 動 元に戻す, 復活させる
- **review** 動 批評する, 視察する
- **rhinoceros** 名 サイ
- **richly** 副 ぜいたくに, 豪華に
- **rise** 熟 give rise to ～を引き起こす
- **Robin Hood: Prince of Thieves** 『ロビン・フッド/プリンス・オブ・ウェールズ』《アメリカ映画, 1991》
- **rocky** 形 岩の多い
- **role** 名 役割
- **roll down** (車などが)走る
- **Roman** 形 ローマ(人)の 名 ローマ人[市民]
- **romantic** 形 ロマンチックな, 空想的な
- **Roots** 『ルーツ』《アメリカの小説, テレビドラマ, 1976》
- **roughly** 副 おおよそ, 概略的に
- **royalty** 名 王族
- **ruin** 名 遺跡, 廃墟, 荒廃
- **ruler** 名 支配者
- **run away** 逃げ出す

S

- **sacred** 形 神聖な, 厳粛な
- **sadly** 副 不幸にも, 悲しいことに
- **Sahara Desert** サハラ砂漠
- **sailor** 名 船員, 船乗り
- **Saint Rupert** 聖ルペルト《ザルツブルクの司教, 660?–710》
- **Saint Virgil** 聖ヴィルギル《ザルツブルクの司教, 700–784》

Word List

- **Salzburg** 名 ザルツブルク《地名》
- **Sana'a** 名 サナア《イエメンの首都》
- **sanctuary** 名 ①聖域, 保護区 ② 《the S-》ザ・サクチュアリ《環状列石の遺跡》
- **sand** 名 砂地
- **scientific** 形 科学の
- **Scottish** 形 スコットランド人の
- **sculpture** 名 彫刻
- **sea anemone** イソギンチャク
- **sea iguana** ウミイグアナ
- **seasonal** 形 季節の
- **select** 動 選び出す, 選定する
- **selection** 名 淘汰
- **sell off** ~を売却する
- **Serengeti National Park** セレンゲッティ国立公園
- **set up** 配置する, 設置する
- **setting** 名 周囲の環境, 状況
- **settled** 形 安定した, 落ち着いた
- **settlement** 名 集落
- **settler** 名 移住者, 入植者
- **Shaanxi Procince** 陝西省《地名》
- **Shah Jahan** シャー・ジャハーン《ムガル帝国の王, 1592–1666》
- **Shakya** 名 釈迦族《古代北インドの一部族》
- **shale** 名 頁岩《泥や粘土鉱物からなる堆積岩》
- **sheet** 名 (水・雪・地層などの)薄い広がり
- **shelter** 名 避難所, 隠れ家 動 避難する, 隠れる
- **Shi Huang** 始皇帝《初めて中国を統一した皇帝, 紀元前259–246》
- **Shinto** 名 神道
- **Shiraito Fall** 白糸の滝
- **Shotoku** 名 聖徳太子《飛鳥時代の皇族, 政治家, 574–622》
- **showcase** 名 陳列棚, ショーケース
- **shrimp** 名 小エビ
- **Siddhartha Gautama** ゴータマ・シッダッタ《仏教の開祖, 紀元前5世紀頃》
- **Siem Reap** シェムリアップ《地名》
- **Silbury Hill** シルベリー・ヒル《人口丘の遺跡》
- **silk** 名 絹(布), 生糸
- **similar to** 《be -》~に似ている
- **simply** 副 単に, ただ
- **since** 熟 ever since それ以来ずっと
- **sink** 動 沈む
- **Siringitu** 名 シリンギトゥ《地名》
- **sit on** ~の上に乗る, ~の上に座っている
- **Six-gun Battery** 六連砲台
- **skeleton** 名 骨格
- **slave** 名 奴隷
- **slowly** 副 ゆっくり
- **snow-cap** 形 雪を頂いた
- **so** 熟 and so それだから, それで so that ~するために, ~できるように so ~ that … 非常に~なので…
- **soaring** 形 空にそびえる
- **society** 名 社会
- **soft-bodied** 形 軟体動物の
- **solitude** 名 孤独, 人里離れた場所
- **Solomon** 名 ソロモン《古代イスラエルの王, 前1011–前901》
- **solstice** 名 (夏至・冬至の)至
- **something of** いくぶん~の気がある
- **sometimes** 副 時々, 時たま
- **Songhai Empire** ソンガイ帝国《かつて西スーダンに存在した王国, 1340–1591》

World Heritage Site Top 38

- **soon** 熟 as soon as ~するとすぐ, ~するや否や
- **southeast** 名 南東(部)
- **southern** 形 南の
- **southwest** 形 南西の
- **Soviet** 名 旧ソビエト連邦
- **Spain** 名 スペイン《国名》
- **Spanish** 形 スペイン(人)の 名 スペイン人
- **species** 名 種, 種類, 人種
- **specific** 形 明確な
- **Sphinx** 名 スフィンクス《ライオンの体と人間の頭部を持つ神話上の生物》
- **spice** 名 スパイス, 香辛料
- **spiritual** 形 精神的な, 霊的な
- **stair** 名《-s》階段, はしご
- **starved** 形 飢えた
- **statue** 名 像
- **stone circle** 環状列石, ストーンサークル
- **Stonehenge** 名 ストーンヘンジ, 環状列石
- **stormy** 形 激しい
- **strategic** 形 戦略上で重要な
- **stretch** 動 広がる, 広げる 名 広がり
- **striking** 形 著しい, 目立つ
- **structure** 名 構造, 建造物
- **stupa** 名 仏舎利塔, 仏塔
- **subspecies** 名 亜種
- **such a** そのような
- **such as** たとえば~, ~のような
- **Suddhodana** 名 シュッドーダナ《釈迦族の王, 釈迦の父》
- **Suiko** 名 推古天皇《飛鳥時代の女性天皇, 554–628》
- **sure** 熟 for sure 確かに make sure 確かめる, 確認する, 確実に~になるようにする
- **surrounding** 形 周囲の
- **survive** 動 生き残る, 存続する
- **swan** 名 ハクチョウ(白鳥)
- **symbol** 名 シンボル, 象徴
- **symbolism** 名 記号体系
- **Syria** 名 シリア《国名》
- **Syrian** 形 シリア(人)の
- **system** 熟 cave system 洞窟

T

- **Taj Mahal** タージ・マハル《墓廟》
- **take ~ back to** ①~を…へ持ち帰る ②~を…に引き戻す
- **take from** ~から引き出す
- **take over** 引き継ぐ, 支配する, 乗っ取る
- **tale** 名 話, 物語 fairy tale おとぎ話
- **Tanzania** 名 タンザニア《国名》
- **tap** 動 蛇口[栓]をつける
- **teaching** 名《-s》教え, 教訓
- **tell of** ~について話す[説明する]
- **temperature** 名 温度
- **temple** 名 寺, 神殿
- **Temple of Athena Nike** アテーナー・ニーケー神殿
- **Terai Plain** タライ平原
- **terrace** 名 段丘, 台地
- **terracotta** 名 赤土素焼き, テラコッタ
- **terror** 名 恐怖
- **than** 熟 more than ~以上
- **then** 熟 by then その時までに
- **thieves** 名 thief (泥棒)の複数
- **this way** このように
- **thousands of** 何千という
- **threaten** 動 おびやかす

Word List

- **thrive** 動 よく育つ, 繁栄する
- **throughout** 前 ①~中, ~を通じて ②~のいたるところに
- **thunder** 動 轟音を立てる
- **Timbuktu** 名 トンブクトゥ《地名》
- **time** 熟 any time いつでも at the time そのころ, 当時の by the time ~する時までに in time やがて of the time 当時の, 当節の over time 時間とともに, そのうち
- **timeless** 形 悠久の
- **tiny** 形 ちっぽけな, とても小さい
- **tomb** 名 墓穴, 墓石, 納骨堂
- **Tongariro National Park** トンガリロ国立公園
- **too ~ to** …するには~すぎる
- **tortoise** 名 カメ(亀)
- **touching** 形 いじらしい, ジーンとくる
- **tourism** 名 観光旅行, 観光業
- **tourist** 名 旅行者, 観光客
- **tower-like** 形 塔のような
- **trader** 名 商人, 貿易業者
- **trading** 名 貿易, 商取引
- **tradition** 名 伝統, しきたり
- **traditional** 形 伝統的な
- **trait** 名 特色, 特徴
- **transport** 動 輸送[運送]する
- **traveler** 名 旅行者
- **treasure** 名 財宝, 貴重品, 宝物
- **treasury** 名 宝物殿
- **trench** 名 (深い)溝
- **tropical** 形 熱帯の
- **truly** 副 全く, 本当に, 真に
- **Tuareg** 名 トゥアレグ人《サハラ砂漠西部の遊牧民族》
- **tunnel** 名 トンネル
- **Turk** 名 トルコ人, トルコ族
- **Turkey** 名 トルコ《国名》
- **Turkish** 形 トルコ(人)の 名 トルコ語
- **turn into** ~に変わる
- **turn out** 結局~であるということが分かる
- **turquoise blue** 青緑色, ターコイズブルー
- **turtle** 名 ウミガメ(海亀)

U

- **U.S.A.** 略 アメリカ合衆国(= United States of America)
- **Umayyad Great Mosque** ウマイヤド・モスク《イスラム教の礼拝堂》
- **unbelievable** 形 信じられない(ほどの)
- **unclean** 形 汚れた
- **undergo** 動 (変化などを)経験する
- **underground** 形 地下の[にある] 副 地下で
- **underwater** 形 水面下の
- **UNESCO** 略 国際連合教育科学文化機関, ユネスコ(= United Nations Educational, Scientific, and Cultural Organization)
- **unify** 動 統一する
- **union** 名 連合, 同盟 World Conservation Union 国際自然保護連合
- **unique** 形 唯一の, ユニークな, 独自の
- **unite** 動 まとめる, 団結させる
- **United Kingdom** 英国, イギリス
- **United Nations Educational, Scientific, and Cultural Organization** 国際自然保護連合, ユネスコ
- **universe** 名 宇宙, 全世界

WORLD HERITAGE SITE TOP 38

- **University of Sankore** サンコーレ大学
- **upper** 形 上の
- **use** 熟 in use 使用されて　used to 以前は~だった, 以前はよく~したものだった
- **Uttar Pradesh** ウッタルプラデシ州《地名》

V

- **valuable** 形 貴重な, 役に立つ
- **vast** 形 広大な, 巨大な, ばく大な
- **Veneti** 名 ウェネティ族《イタリア半島北東部に住んでいた人々》
- **venetian** 名 ヴェネチア市民 形 ヴェネチアの
- **Venice** 名 ヴェネチア, ヴェニス《イタリアの都市》
- **Victoria Falls** ヴィクトリアの滝
- **Vincent van Gogh** ヴィンセント・ヴァン・ゴッホ《オランダの画家, 1853-1890》
- **visible** 形 見ることのできる
- **visitor** 名 訪問客
- **volcanic** 形 火山の
- **volcano** 名 火山, 噴火口

W

- **Wailing Wall** 嘆きの壁《エルサレム神殿の外壁》
- **walk across** ~を歩いて渡る
- **war** 動 戦争をする, 争う 名 戦争, 武力闘争　civil war 内戦, 内乱　Hundred Years' War 百年戦争《1337-1453》
- **warehouse** 名 倉庫
- **warrior** 名 戦士, 軍人
- **watch over** 見守る, 見張る
- **waterfall** 名 滝
- **way** 熟 in this way このようにして　on one's way to ~に行く途中で　this way このように　way to ~する方法
- **weapon** 名 武器, 兵器
- **Wei** 名 魏《中国戦国時代に存在した国, 前403-前225》
- **weigh** 動 重さが~ある
- **well** 名 井戸 熟 as well なお, その上, 同様に　as well as ~と同様に, ~に加えて
- **well-designed** 形 優れた設計の
- **Wessex** 名 ウェセックス王国《イングランドにかつて存在した王国, 6世紀-1016》
- **West Kennet Long Barrow** ウェスト・ケネット・ロング・バロウ《巨石建造物の遺跡》
- **western** 形 ①西の, 西側の ②《W-》西洋の
- **wetness** 名 湿気
- **whether** 接 ~であろうとなかろうと　whether or not ~かどうか
- **which** 熟 all of which ~の中で　of which ~の中で
- **while** 熟 for a while しばらくの間, 少しの間
- **wildebeest** 名 ヌー
- **wilderness** 名 荒野, 荒れ地
- **Wiltshire County** ウィルトシャー州
- **wind through** ~を曲がりくねって進む
- **Windmill Hill** ウィンドミル・ヒル文化《イギリス南東部の新石器時代最古の文化, 前3500頃-前2500頃》
- **witness** 動 目撃する, ~に立ち会う
- **Wolfgang Amadeus Mozart** ヴォルファング・アマデウス・モーツァルト《作曲家, 1756-91》

Word List

- **wood-block print** 木版画
- **wooden** 形 木製の, 木でできた
- **Woodhenge** 名 ウッドヘンジ《環状木柱列の遺跡》
- **work** 熟 work in 〜の分野で働く work of 〜の仕事, 作品 work on 〜で働く, 〜に取り組む, 〜に影響を与える works of art 芸術作品
- **World Conservation Union** 国際自然保護連合
- **World Heritage Site** 世界遺産
- **world-class** 形 国際的レベルの, 世界に名の通った
- **world-famous** 形 世界的に有名な
- **worse** 形 いっそう悪い, よりひどい
- **worshipper** 名 礼拝者
- **worst** 形 《the –》最も悪い
- **writing** 名 書かれたもの, 文書

X

- **Xi'an** 名 西安《地名》

Y

- **Yakushi Nyorai Buddha** 薬師如来菩薩《大乗仏教の如来の一尊》
- **Yamuna River** ヤムナー川
- **Yemen** 名 イエメン《国名》
- **Yemenite** 名 イエメン人
- **Yoho** 名 ヨーホー《地名》
- **Yomei** 名 用明天皇《飛鳥時代の天皇, ?–587》

Z

- **Zambezi River** ザンベジ川
- **Zambia** 名 ザンビア《国名》
- **zebra** 名 シマウマ
- **Zimbabwe** 名 ジンバブエ《国名》

ラダーシリーズ
World Heritage Site Top 38 世界遺産ベスト38

2015年8月18日　第1刷発行

著　者　ニーナ・ウェグナー

発行者　浦　晋亮

発行所　IBCパブリッシング株式会社
　　　　〒162-0804 東京都新宿区中里町29番3号
　　　　菱秀神楽坂ビル9F
　　　　Tel. 03-3513-4511　Fax. 03-3513-4512
　　　　www.ibcpub.co.jp

© IBC Publishing, Inc. 2015

印刷　株式会社シナノパブリッシングプレス
装丁　伊藤 理恵　カバーイラスト　sdecoret/Shutterstock.com
組版データ　Sabon Roman + DIN Next LT Pro Bold Condensed

落丁本・乱丁本は、小社宛にお送りください。送料小社負担にてお取り替えいたします。本書の無断複写（コピー）は著作権法上での例外を除き禁じられています。

Printed in Japan
ISBN978-4-7946-0363-0